A PICTORIAL ENCYCLOPEDIA

OF CIVIL WAR MEDICAL INSTRUMENTS AND EQUIPMENT

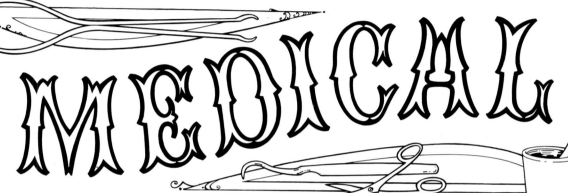

DR. GORDON DAMMANN

D1422021

PICTORIAL HISTORIES PUBLISHING COMPANY
MISSOULA, MONTANA

COPYRIGHT © 1983 GORDON DAMMANN

All rights reserved. No part of this book
may be used or reproduced without written
permission of the publisher.

LIBRARY OF CONGRESS
CATALOG CARD NUMBER 83-80357

ISBN 0-933126-32-8

First Printing: April 1983
Second Printing: March 1984
Third Printing: April 1985
Fourth Printing: April 1987
Fifth Printing: March 1989
Sixth Printing: August 1990
Seventh Printing: April 1992
Eighth Printing: July 1993
Ninth Printing: February 1995
Tenth Printing: June 1996

Typography: Arrow Graphics
Layout: Stan Cohen

Albumen Print showing what appears
to be three surgeons and a nurse
treating a soldier.

PICTORIAL HISTORIES PUBLISHING COMPANY
713 South Third West
Missoula, Montana 59801

CONTENTS

CDV and autograph of Surgeon
General William A. Hammond. Hammond served from 1861-1864.

Surgeon General Samuel Moore C.S.A.
He served the Confederate States as
Head of its Medical Dept. for the dura-
tion of the war.

PREFACE

What will a book about the instruments and equipment used by the medical and dental professions during the Civil War try to accomplish? It *will not* try to explain the whole medical knowledge of the 1860s. The fine books already published by Brooks, Adams and Cunningham have done that. This work will bring collectors and dealers of medical antiquities some insight as to what was used and how the equipment was used. All too often instruments have been mis-named or mis-labelled, and I hope this publication will clarify this area. This will not be the final volume of this treatise. As different examples are brought forward, subsequent volumes will be issued.

Since Volume I of *Pictorial Encyclopedia of Civil War Medical Instruments and Equipment* was presented in 1983, over 500 copies have been sold. As mentioned in the Preface of Volume I, when different examples of medical items were uncovered, additional volumes would be forthcoming. Thus Volume II has been written.

As with most things man has done, Volume I needs to be corrected and revised in the following areas:

Illust. 87 (page 56). The screw tops of the vials indicate this to be post Civil War.

Illust. 88 (page 56). The bottle marked "South Carolina Dispensary" is definitely post Civil War.

Illust. 155 (page 81). This was not a hat device, but an insignia from medical epulettes.

Illust. 163 and 179 (pages 84 and 89). The book is one and the same.

Illust. 182 (page 91). The Hospital Day Book is from the hospital on Broad & Cherry streets in Philadelphia, not Baltimore.

Illust. on page 98. The dimensions of this hospital flag are 110 inches long by 58 inches wide. The green "H" is 24½ inches high and 17½ inches wide. Thanks to Seward R. Osborne for the information and picture.

ACKNOWLEDGEMENTS

After all is done and the author reflects upon all who have helped him in his search, a good feeling has to come over him. If it were not for family and friends, the project would not have been completed.

This book is dedicated to my wife, Karen, and my two sons, Greg and Doug, who have supported me with their love. Karen has spent countless hours typing and retyping—giving me a shoulder to cry on when it seemed all was going wrong. Greg and Doug gave me their understanding when I spent time researching and writing instead of playing.

Also to my father and mother, to my inlaws who I consider likened to my own parents, who taught me the value of hard work and perserverance, I say thank you.

Many friends have lent support during this endeavor: My partner and his wife, Dr. and Mrs. Robert Ziegler, were always there with encouragement and a martini when needed; Mark Johnson has ridden with me for many miles to and from Civil War shows and has been a tremendous help in acquiring books and manuscripts; Dave Franz, a Civil War music scholar, has put up with many nights of music, rehashing and Peleg; Fritz Werhane, my roommate on the Chicago Roundtable trips; fellow collectors, Dr. Tom Wheat, Jim Brady, Mike Cunningham, Dr. Tom Sweeney, Dr. Mark Griffith, George Lower, Dale Anderson, Jim Stametelos, Neil Weinstein, Tom Brinkmeier, John Heflen, Dr. Sam Kirkpatrick, Charles Rhodes III, and Edgar Archer. All have shared a wealth of knowledge with me.

A particular thank you to Dan Weinberg of the Abraham Lincoln Book Shop and to John Paul of Prairie Archives Book Shop who have kept me supplied with medical books of the 1860s. Also to Ms. Jeri Strohecker for proofreading the manuscript at 3 o'clock in the morning.

To all these people and many more known only to me, many thanks and may the knowledge and friendship we have shared be habit forming.

CHAPTER ONE

SURGICAL PROCEDURES

Probably the most striking of all the medical equipment is the large amputation kit. Every museum or Civil War display has one. The most often-heard comment is, "Oh! Isn't that gruesome." Yes, it is gruesome, but very necessary to the operating surgeon. The most common surgical procedure of the war was amputation. It was the accepted medical treatment in the 1860s for a gunshot wound to an extremity. Documenting this is the Sanitary Commission's report published in 1861:

> In army practice, on the field, amputation, when necessary ought to be primary. Patients, in most cases, cannot bear removal from the field without increased danger, neither can they have afterwards the hygienic attentions which secondary amputations most necessarily require, therefore:
>
> 1. Amputate with as little delay as possible after the receipt of the injury in those cases where there is intensive suffering from the presence in the wound of bone spicule or other foreign bodies, which the fingers or forceps cannot reach.
>
> 2. In those cases where a limb is nearly torn off, and a dangerous hemorrhage is occurring which cannot be arrested.
>
> 3. In army practice, attempts to save a limb which might be perfectly successful in civil life, cannot be made. Especially in this case in compound gunshot fractures of the thigh, bullet wounds of the knee joint and similar injuries to the leg, in which, at first sight, amputation may not seem necessary. Under such circumstances attempts to preserve the limb will be followed by extreme local and constitutional disturbance. Conservative surgery is here in error; in order to save life, the limb must be sacrificed."[1]

In the same light, Dr. Eric Carver in his paper on orthopedic surgery during the Civil War gives his reasons why the primary amputation was accepted therapy. He states that the primary amputation, done within 24 hours after receiving the wound, reduced the high rate of infection, saved lives from septicemia and provided a rapid, efficient means for the treatment of many thousands of casualties. Statistics reveal that the mortality for the primary amputation was 28 percent, but if the surgery were delayed the mortality rate rose to 52 percent.[2]

D.J. Julian Chisolm in his "Manual of Military Surgery for the Surgeons of the Confederate States Army" states "that the rule in military surgery is absolute, viz: that the amputating knife should immediately follow the condemnation of the limb. These are operations of the battlefield, and should be performed at the field infirmary. When this golden opportunity, before reaction, is lost, it can never be compensated for."[3]

With the preceding information we can set to rest the notion that the Civil War surgeon was a knife-and saw-happy butcher who saw great piles of amputated limbs as his claim to fame. Medical knowledge of the era dictated that this means of saving lives—the amputation—was the soldiers' best hope for survival. Realizing that the primary amputation was the accepted mode of treatment during the Civil War, we should examine the anatomical sites of the amputations and different techniques for performing the surgery. All authors of the period agree that the farther away from the trunk of the body, the greater the patient's chance of survival. Carver shows this in the following table:

CASES OF UNION AMPUTATIONS 29,990[4]			
	Cases	Deaths	Percent of Fatalities
Fingers	7,900	198	3
Forearm	1,700	245	14
Upper Arm	6,500	1,273	24
Toes	1,500	81	6
Lower Leg	5,500	1,700	38
Middle Thigh	6,300	3,411	54
Knee Joint	195	111	58
Hip Joint	66	55	88

Also by saving as much of the extremity as possible, the patient would be able to have a more functional arm or leg to work with. Rule of thumb for the Civil War surgeon: save as much of the limb as possible.

Smith's *A System of Operative Surgery*, published in 1856, describes three different techniques for amputation—the flap operation and the circular operation. The circular technique is the oldest method of operating, dating to the time of Celsus. In this technique the skin was incised with the Lister Knives and the soft tissue drawn back by a retractor or the hands of an available assistant. The bone was cut transversely across and the operation completed by tying off the arteries, replacing the cuff of skin and applying bandages.

The other technique is described as the oval method. It was the same as the circular except that the cut was made a little higher on one side of the limb than on the other, thus forming an oval instead of a circular wound. This type of operation lent itself to amputation through the joint capsule.

In the flap technique a V-shaped cut was made either from skin to bone or from bone outward to the skin. Smith states that the flap operation was preferred by some surgeons because it could be performed rapidly. Its drawback was the susceptibility to secondary hemorrhage.

Dr. Frank Hamilton in his *Treatise of Military Surgery and Hygiene* stated that "whatever method of amputation is adopted, there is one thing upon which we desire to insist, as of paramount importance—namely, that the bone should be well dissected up before it is severed. The length of the flap is always of less consequence than the depth at which the section of bone is made underneath the mass of flesh. In order to accomplish this, it is our practice to apply the retractor firmly, girdle the bone closely with the knife, and then with the thumbnails or the handle of the knife, peel up the periosteum freely an inch or more. In addition to the value of this practice in the point of view already considered, it is possible that it may be of service by retaining a sort of periosteal flap or covering for the end of the bone."[5] The surgeons were looking for a large area of tissue to cover the stump of bone to insure good healing and to insure that an acceptable replacement device could be constructed upon it.

Dr. Chisolm states quite emphatically in his manual: "In dividing the skin, the surgeon cannot be too careful to leave an ample flap to cover the heads of the bones. This is the first rule in amputation."[6]

The following illustrations show how and when certain instruments were used during the amputation procedure. Let us go through the procedure step by step:

The soldier requiring the amputation would be brought to the operating table, which in some cases was nothing more than wood planks set upon saw-horses or large barrels. Anything that would support the weight of a man was used, including tables and church pews.

The next step of the operation is probably the least understood. During the Civil War the surgeons did use general anesthetics to render the patient surgically unconscious. The anesthetics were chloroform and ether (Illust. 89 and 91). Anesthetics have been used in this country since the 1840s. There are four claimants to the title of founder of surgical anesthesia. They are Crawford W. Long and Charles T. Jackson, physicians, and Horace Wells and T.G. Morton, dentists.[7] It is not our purpose to debate who actually founded the use of anesthesia but only to state that both chloroform and ether were used. Dr. James Syme in his *Principals and Practice of Surgery*, written in 1858, gives his observations on the use of anesthetics: "There can now be no question as to the utility and humanity of using chloroform in most surgical operations. Anesthetics are, in reality, as safe a remedy as any we use, provided they are used properly. Pure chloroform is preferred by me to either ether or chloric ether....The secret of success consists in affording the patient a due supply of natural air while inhaling the chloroform....The stomach of the patient should be empty and his mind at a state of rest."[8] Syme is not describing wartime surgery and this last thought would be impossible to achieve in a battlefield situation. The proper thinking was there to use.

Syme continues, "If the pulse sinks too much, the patient should have a smell of liquor of ammonia."[9] Since many of the battlefield operations were performed outside, the death from anesthetic overdose was quite negligible even though chloroform was the substance used. Today chloroform is not used as an anesthetic because it is quite toxic. Another factor contributing to the small percentage of deaths from anesthetics was that most surgical procedures were carried out in a short amount of time. An amputation of an arm or leg could be finished in less than fifteen minutes. The patient, therefore, was under the influence of chloroform or ether for a short time and the toxicity would not have a chance to build to a dangerous level.

As soon as the patient was "surgically asleep" the blood to the site would be stopped by either a tourniquet (Illust. 28) or, as most surgeons wanted, by the hands of a competent assistant. Then the skin was incised with a large amputating knife (Illust. 20), or if a flap technique was employed, with a catlin knife (Illust. 21). The skin would be retracted and the muscle tissue would be incised with the large knives. The bone would be exposed and dissected back with a bone scraper or raspatory (Illust. 14). The surgical saw was used to cut the bone (Illust. 6). The surgeon would next ligate the major blood vessels by use of surgical silk thread (Illust. 27). To facilitate the grasping of the arteries, a tenaculum (Illust. 25) or an artery forceps (Illust. 12) would be used. After the blood vessels were tied and the major bleeding stopped, a gnawing forceps (Illust. 15) or bone file (Illust. 10) would be used to smooth the stump of bone. This would eliminate future sequestra of bone, and the healing process was much quicker. The wound was closed with silk thread and curved needles (Illust. 27). Surgeon Chisolm explains the operation in these terms:

> In performance of all serious operations there should be three assistants. One aide gives the chloroform, a second compresses the main artery (Chisolm detested the use of tourniquets and probes) and a third holds the limb and supports the flap during the section. The aide who administers the chloroform during the incisions, can assist in ligating arteries....Having assigned the aides their posts and seen that all necessary instruments which may be needed are on hand—for a surgeon should never commence an operation until he has satisfied himself on this score—the surgeon removes the limb, ligates the vessels and when all oozing has ceased, secures the stump by points of suture placed at intervals of one inch or a little less along the entire length of the wound."[10]

After the operation the patient would be fanned to purge his lungs of the anesthetic. A quick smell of liquor of ammonia would be used to obtain consciousness. If the patient still did not respond, the surgeon had a unique way of jolting the patient's system to awaken him—chloroform would be splashed onto the patient's scrotum, causing an immediate reaction of cold. The subject of post-operative pain and how the Civil War surgeon alleviated it will be discussed in another chapter.

Other Civil War surgical techniques should also be discussed. The large amputation kit had instruments that were used for resections, sometimes called exsections, trephining, and simple gunshot wounds. By definition a resection is an operation that removes a sufficient portion of the bone structure that was damaged, but retains the limb.[11] The result is a shortened limb with restricted movement or function, but it still is present and will allow the patient some use. This operation required the surgeon to have much more knowledge of anatomy and refinement of manual skills; it also put a strain on the patient because of the length of the procedure. Also required were specific instruments that were not used for other techniques, such as various saws, chisels and bone-nippers. Probably the most specialized instrument was the chain saw

(Illust. 7). The flexible saw blade was removed from one of its handles and passed around the bone to be resected; it was connected back to its handle, and a push-pull motion cut the bone from the backside forward. Smaller saws, such as the metacarpal saw (Illust. 8), were also used in this type of procedure. Surgeons used a straight or gnawing forceps to grasp the resected bone (Illust. 18). Dr. Edward Warren, in 1863, wrote in his *Epitome of Practical Surgery for Field and Hospital* the rules for resections:

> 1. Distinguish well the anatomical relations of the parts before commencing the operation. Know where the nerves and vessels are to be found, for it is exceedingly difficult to distinguish them during the operation.
>
> 2. In addition to the ordinary instruments, have on hand a cutting forceps, a gauge, a mallet, and saws of different sizes and shapes.
>
> 3. Open a free way to the bone, but expose as little as possible of the muscles and tendons.
>
> 4. The nerves, the veins, and arterial trunks are never to be divided; while the tendons, as a general thing, must be preserved.
>
> 5. Before employing the saw, ascertain to what extent the bone is diseased and see that the soft tissues are well out of the way of the injury.
>
> 6. Remove completely every part touched by the disease or reached by the injury.
>
> 7. Cut off the bones connected with the articulations at the same distance from the joint.
>
> 8. Preserve as much of the periosteum and take away as large a portion of the synovial membrane as practicable.
>
> 9. When the lower limb has been operated upon, bring the bone together and extend it, but when an upper, put it in a state of semi flexion, and leave the bones a little apart so as to secure, if possible, an artificial joint.
>
> 10. Make the incision on the side opposite to the main arteries.
>
> 11. Make the existing wound lie, if possible, in the line of one of the incisions, which should be so arranged as to permit the free drainage of pus.[12]

All medical authors of the 1860s agreed that this operation should not be attempted unless the surgeon and the patient were prepared for it. The surgeon had to have sufficient skill and *time* to give to this procedure. The patient had to be strong enough to undergo the extra time of operation and recuperation necessary for the success of the procedure. The condition of the patient's surroundings were also very important. The hospital had to be fixed, and sanitation and ventilation had to be above the normal.

Illust. 9 and 11 show instruments that were used for the procedure called trephining. This type of surgery, done primarily on the skull, dates back to Egyptian times. Evidence of this procedure can be found in the mummies of ancient Egypt. It was used as a treatment for severe headaches. The procedure involved simply drilling a small hole in the skull bone or cranium to relieve the pressure of underlying hemorrhage. It is also used to treat a depressed fracture of the cranium. The proper technique for using the trephine was to introduce the central bit beyond the level of saw edges. After the bit was firmly secured by sliding screws on the side of the instrument, the bone was engaged with a semicircular motion. Then the central bit was retracted and a circular motion was used to finish cutting through the bone. An elevator was used to separate the circular piece from the rest of the skull. In the hands of an inexperienced surgeon this instrument was deadly. In fact some surgeons (Chisolm of the CSA) advocated the complete disuse of the trephine. The principle of the trephine was solid, but the use of an unsterilized instrument on the brain cavity was an invitation for disaster.

The human body, however, is sometimes able to withstand much abuse as can be seen in the case of Private Edmond Gordon. He was shot while on picket duty near Yorktown, Virginia, on September 18, 1862. "The ball broke into the skull near the anterior inferior angle of the parietal bone of the left side. He remained all night on the ground. When he reached the hospital he was unable to speak but he seemed conscious and could walk. The loss of the power of speech, together with the depression of the fragment, seemed to authorize the use of the trephine. After having removed a circular piece of bone, and while lifting the depressed fragments, the left side of his face became violently convulsed but this ceased when the fragment was removed. A pretty free hemorrhage, which immediately occurred from the middle meningeal artery, ceased spontaneously in a few minutes, apparently from the pressure of the brain within. Two days after we found him doing well, but we have not heard from him since."[13]

The next major surgical procedure of the Civil War was treatment of the gunshot wound. Dr. Carver states in his paper that war losses from gunshot wounds were 400,000 and of these, 204,000 died. He also states that 35.1 percent of these were arm wounds, and 35.7 percent were leg wounds.[14] Treatment for all these wounds was basically the same. The bullet, if located, was to be extracted. The major blood vessels would have to be sutured, the wound bandaged. With the introduction of the conical projectile, the severity of the wound would be greatly increased. The round ball used early in the war, primarily by Confederate forces, would tend to bounce off tissue rather than bore through it. The trauma to deeper tissue was lessened. But with the introduction of the conical or "minie ball," the wound was found to be more severe. Instead of bouncing off tissue, either muscle or bone, the wedge of the conical ball would bore through the area and usually rest near the opposite side of the body from its point of entrance. "The explanation of this fact is simple. The skin is tough and elastic, and a missle which has force enough to penetrate it upon one side, has usually sufficient force to transverse to adjacent tissue, while it may not be capable of penetrating again the skin upon the opposite side."[15]

To locate the bullet, the finger technique was most efficient. With the use of the finger came a degree of touch that was lost with the use of a probe. Also, the finger was less likely to damage anatomic structures (arteries and nervous tissue). If the finger was useless because of the wound's position, the bullet probe was used. These are shown in Illust. 26 and 36. Dr. Hamilton describes the use of the probe..."The probe should be seized lightly in the fingers and allowed to drop into the wound rather than be thrust in violently, by which latter method the surgeon will only make new channels, while if his instrument is really in the right direction it will advance toward the ball almost by its own weight. The probe of Nelaton is often invaluable in determining whether the foreign body, the presence of which the ordinary silver prober may discover, is lead or bone. This instrument is a small ball of polished porcelain fastened to the end of the probe."[16] After the foreign body had been located, a variety of forceps could be used in the extraction. Illust. 13, 19, 36, and 37 show the different types used by Civil War surgeons. Of all the forceps shown, the ones listed as Illust. 13 and 36 caused the least trauma to surrounding tissue. The ideal forceps were very thin, with sharp beaks to engage the metal. The Moses forceps (Illust. 36) probably would have been the choice instrument. Its only drawback was a tendency to clog. It is also necessary to remember that the lead projectile would be deformed, and the "cup" shaped forceps would not accommodate this type of foreign body easily. The "pincer" type forceps were also well adapted for removing pieces of clothing from the wound. It must be remembered that any foreign body, such as metal, cloth, or wood, would act as a focus of infection resulting in poor healing. Pieces of shrapnel were easily removed with pincer forceps also.

The natural transition from the preceding topic

would be a discussion on the causes and arresting of hemorrhage. A statement made by Dr. Hamilton bears repeating. "It is one peculiar feature of gunshot injuries that in proportion to the number and severity of the accidents, profuse arterial hemorrhage is rare."[17] This statement makes sense because most of the wounds inflicted were contusions or lacerations, and very seldom incisions. Contused and lacerated arteries retract and form a "shut off valve" rather than bleeding profusely. Soldiers rarely bled to death on the battlefield. There were exceptions, and the most well-known was Albert Sidney Johnston, General of the Confederate forces at Shiloh. He happened to receive a gunshot wound to the back of the knee joint which severed the major artery in that area. He bled to death in a matter of minutes. The wound he received severed the artery rather than crushing it. There were many exceptions to the general rule.

Most of the hemorrhages that occurred during the Civil War can be classified in two categories—primary and secondary. Primary hemorrhage occurred at the time the wound was inflicted; secondary hemorrhage was a complication of surgical procedures.

The best treatment of primary hemorrhage during the Civil War was ligation and moist bandaging. The term ligation means that the larger arteries to the afflicted area would be tied off, usually with surgical silk thread (Illust. 27). The thick-walled arteries would be grasped by either the Olive Point artery forceps (Illust. 12), or the sharp pointed tenaculum (Illust. 25). The artery would be drawn out, and the ligature would be passed around it and tied off. To facilitate the procedure, pressure would be exerted by either hand pressure or a tourniquet to close off the blood supply to this artery. After the ligature was secure, it would be tested by releasing the hand pressure on the tourniquet to see if the blood flow had stemmed.

Venous blood flow would be stemmed by exerting pressure with bandage material, such as the adhesive plaster bandage (Illust. 47). Cautery is sometimes mentioned in the literature, but it was rarely used. Chemical styptics were employed. These compounds were nitrate of silver, sulphate of copper, alum, tannic acid, tincture of ferric chloride, and "matico" in either leaf or tincture, nearly all of which act by constricting the vessel. Hemorrhage could also be arrested by applying either fine sponge or dry lint to favor clot formation at the end of the vessel. These compounds, when combined with pressure, occasionally served a good purpose.[18]

Secondary hemorrhage was probably the most deadly. It occurred from the 5th to the 30th day.[19] This hemorrhage was caused by the sloughing of tissue and the giving way of vessels where the ligatures were tied. The surgeon would then have to act quickly and decisively to stem this complication. Usually he would try to tie off the artery above the area of slough. He would use pressure and styptics that were mentioned previously.

In ending this discussion of surgery during the Civil War it is necessary to cover the subject of pain control during surgery. Most surgical manuals of the late 1850s and 1860s ignore this subject, but Surgeon Chisolm of the Confederate Medical Corps devotes much thought to the subject: "Opium, by which we can effect this subjection, will ever be the greatest boon to the military surgeon; it is a remedy which should never be absent from his reach. Going on the field, he should have his pockets well stored with it for immediate use; and in the entire treatment of the wounded it will ever hold a conspicuous place. Morphine is perhaps the best article for wounded men, as it has lost in the preparation some of those astringent properties which, as opium or laudanum, would produce too great a tendency to constipation."[20]

The routes of administration of opium or morphine are three-fold. It could be given through the stomach, usually mixed with water or "spiritus fermenti." The technique was rather slow-acting and caused vomiting problems. Another method applied powder directly into the wound. The surgeon would wet his finger, place the powder on it, and place it on the wound. The third route was the most revolutionary for the period. A Wood's endermic syringe was used. Usually one-half grain of morphine was mixed with three or four drops of water and injected under the skin.

Chisolm gives a case history to illustrate this new technique. "Mr. M. was accidentally shot in the neck with a Colt's pocket revolver. His head being turned, the ball entered the skin over the larynx, coursed downward and backward through the posterior triangle of the neck, and was found under the skin of the shoulder over the spine of the scapula, and removed. Considerable swelling followed, which, diffusing itself, discolored that side of the neck. Some of the brachial plexus of the nerves must have been injured, as the patient was soon seized with violent pain, shooting down toward the fingers...Gum opium and morphine in large doses gave him no relief. The arm was so sensitive that he would not permit it to be handled. One-fourth of a grain of morphine, in three to four drops of water, was injected under the skin of the shoulder; in five minutes all pain had left him and his arm could be examined...."[21]

A whole new area of pain control was dawning in the 1860s. Before this time patients had to endure the immense physical discomfort of injury, and now, because of the Civil War, they had the benefits of pain-killing compounds. To summarize the surgical treatment of the Civil War, we should remember:

1. Amputation was the accepted medical treatment for the majority of gunshot wounds.

2. Anesthetics were used to render the patient surgically unconscious. These agents were chloroform and ether.

3. The surgeon had to operate quickly, usually in less than 15 minutes.

4. New types of operations, such as resection, were developed because of the Civil War.

5. Pain-killing substances such as morphine and opium were used extensively by the surgeons.

Illust. 1 U.S. ARMY STAFF SURGEON'S CAPITAL OPERATING CASE
Dimensions: 43½ cm × 19½ cm × 10 cm
Mahogany case with brass
Marked: U.S.A. Hosp. Dept.

SURGEON'S OPERATING CASE

Illust. 2 Opposite Top
Exposing interior shelf and lining
Marked: "H. Hernstein" plus American Eagle design
Maroon velvet

Illust. 3 Opposite Bottom
In open position, exposing top and middle shelf.

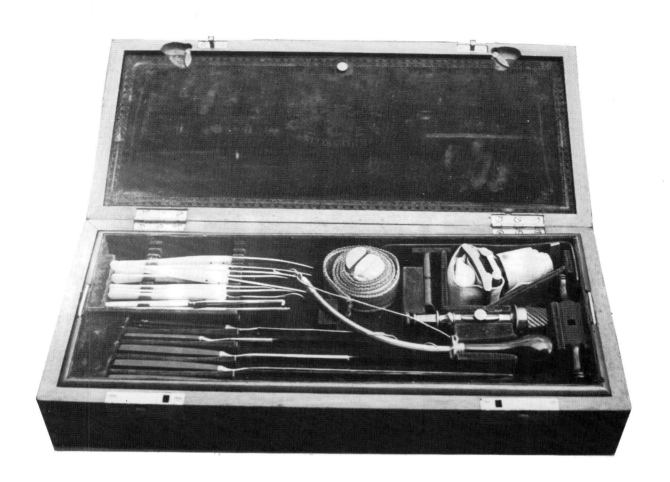

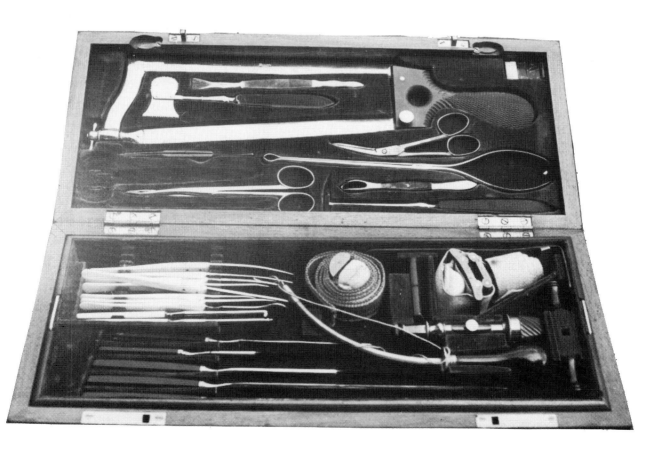

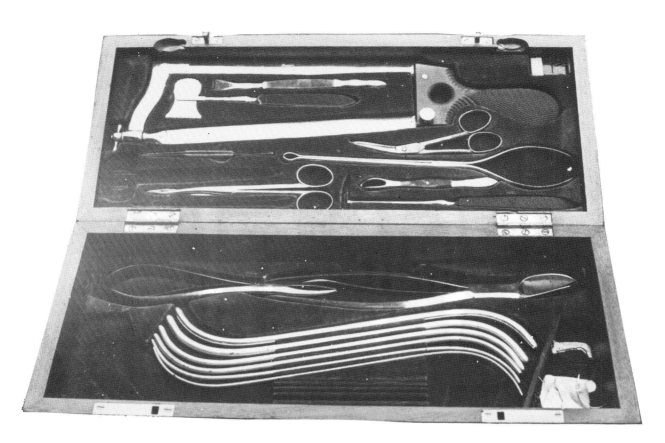

Illust. 4 SURGEON'S OPERATING CASE
In open position, exposing top and bottom shelf.

Illust. 5 BLACK LEATHER CARRYING CASE
Used to carry U.S. Army Staff Surgeon's Operating Case.

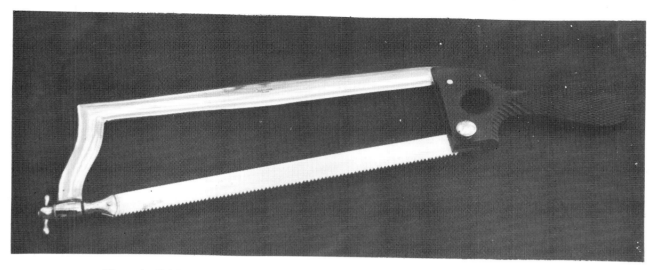

Illust. 6 CAPITAL SAW

Dimensions: 39½ cm × 10 cm.
Marked: Hernstein & Son
The handle is ebony and it features an interchangeable blade.
Use: Cutting through the larger bones of legs and arms during amputation procedure.

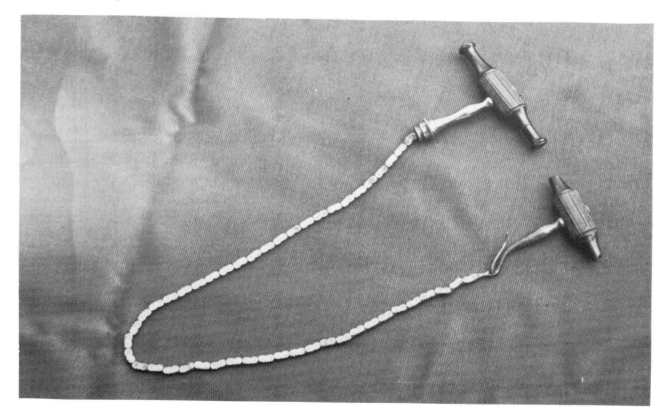

Illust. 7 CHAIN SAW

Dimensions: 41 cm - including two ebony handles (one removable).
Use: For cutting through bone where its location would render it inaccessible to a blade saw. Principally used for resection operations.

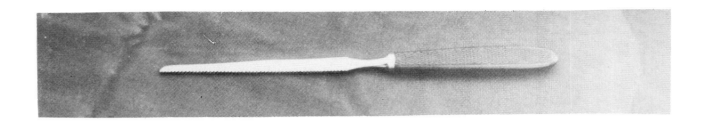

Illust. 8 METACARPAL SAW

Dimensions: 21½ cm
The handle is ebony.
Use: Cutting through smaller bones such as the rib, finger, toe, ankle, or wrist.

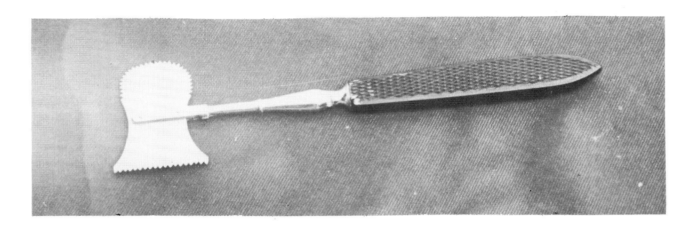

Illust. 9 HEY'S SAW

Dimensions: 16½ cm
The handle is ebony
Marked: Hernstein & Son
Use: Tool used in trephine operation on the skull to reduce fractures of bones of the skull.

Illust. 10 BONE FILE

Dimensions: 10½ cm
Marked: Hernstein & Son
Use: Removal of rough edges of bone after cutting by a saw. These rough spicules would hinder healing and caused infection.

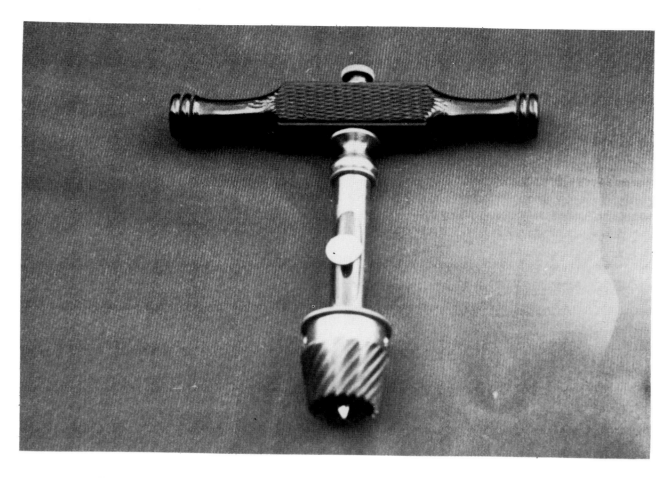

Illust. 11 TREPHINE-CONICAL CROWN

Dimensions: 10½ cm
The handle is ebony.
Use: The principal use in operations of the skull to reduce fractures and also to relieve intercranial pressure due to hemorrhage. Action is that of a drill. It has a limiting bayonet which can be seen extending at the bottom of the drill.

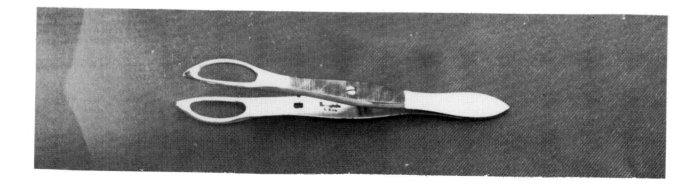

Illust. 12 ARTERY FORCEPS - OLIVE POINT

Dimensions: 12 cm
Marked: Hernstein & Son
Use: For grasping arteries without injury to arterial wall.

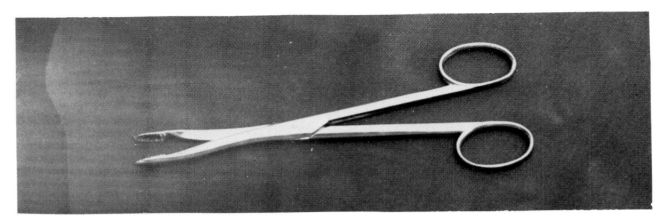

Illust. 13 BONE FORCEPS OR SEQUESTRUM FORCEPS

Dimensions: 16 cm
Use: For removing loose pieces of bone that could cause infection.

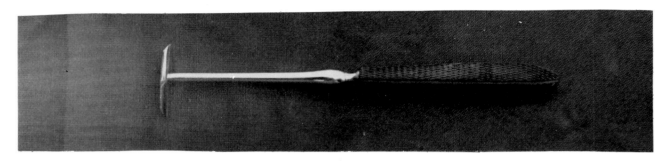

Illust. 14 BONE SCRAPER OR RASPATORY

Dimensions: 19 cm
Use: For scraping necrotic or dead sequestra of bone.

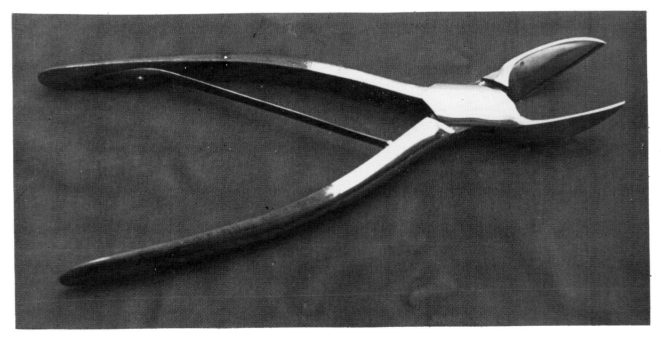

Illust. 15 CURVED GNAWING FORCEPS OR RONGEUR

Dimensions: 26 cm
Use: For contouring stumps of bone and removing rough edges.

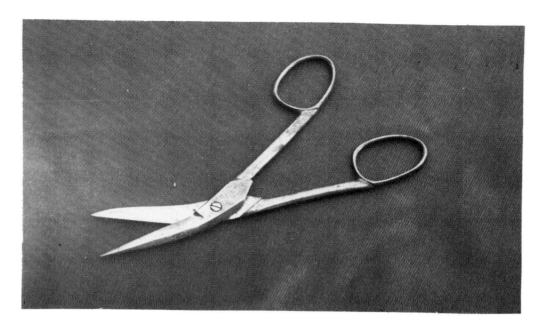

Illust. 16 SCISSORS - CURVED

Dimensions: 13 cm
Use: For cutting tissue, also used for cutting bandage material.

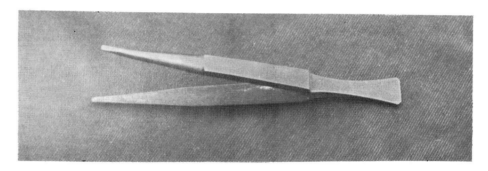

Illust. 17 DISSECTION FORCEPS (Tissue)

Dimensions: 11½ cm
Use: For grasping and holding tissue during operative procedures.

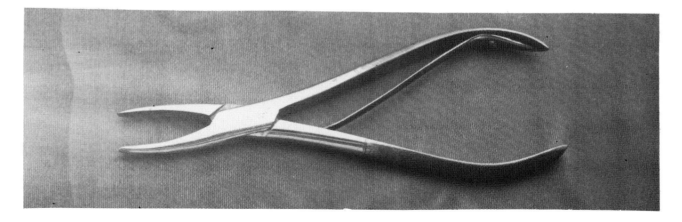

Illust. 18 STRAIGHT GNAWING FORCEPS OR RONGEUR

Dimensions: 20 cm
Use: For removing rough bony edges on the stump after an amputation.

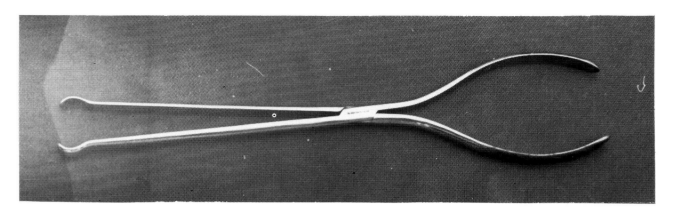

Illust. 19 STRAIGHT FORCEPS - BULLET EXTRACTORS

Dimensions: 25 cm
Marked: Hernstein & Son
Use: For removing lead projectiles. May also be used for removing shrapnel.
The inner part of the curved beaks are serrated.

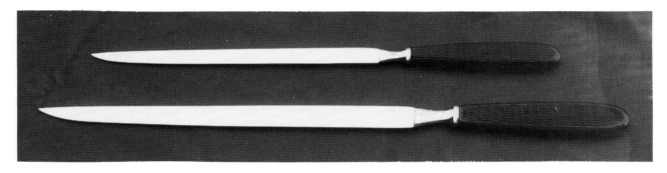

Illust. 20 AMPUTATING KNIVES

Top knife: Amputating knife of medium size. 32½ cm in length.
Bottom knife: Amputating knife of large size. 38½ cm in length.
Use: For cutting or incising soft tissue during the amputation. The first cut would
be through the skin only. The skin would then be reflected and a second cut
would be made through muscle tissue. These were used for the most part in the
Circular Amputation Technique.

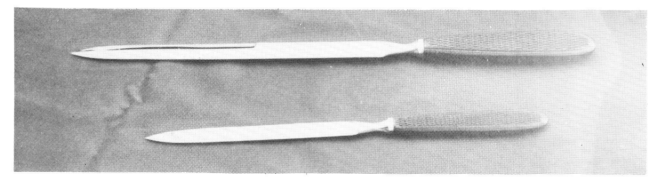

Illust. 21 CATLINS

Top: Large Catlin, 31½ cm in length.
Bottom: Medium Catlin, 23½ cm in length.
The handles are ebony.
Use: These are double-edged knives whereas the amputating knives had a cutting
edge on one side only. The Catlin was used in the Flap Type of amputation
procedure.

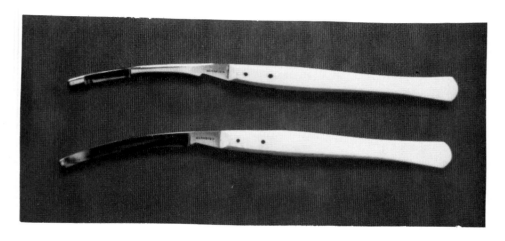

Illust. 22 CURVED BISTOURIES OR HERNIA KNIVES

Dimensions of both: 16½ cm
Marked: Hernstein & Son
Use: A Bistoury is a longer and more slender scalpel. Some have a blunt end (as pictured) so they could be used in wounds without danger of puncturing vital organs.

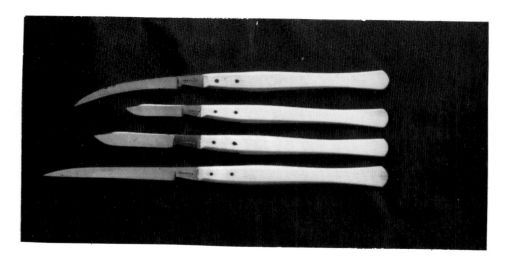

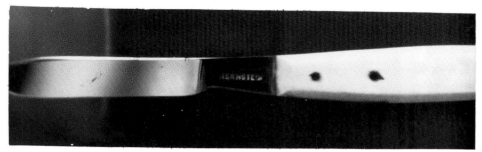

Illust. 23 SURGICAL SCALPELS - Assorted sizes and shapes

Top to bottom in dimensions: 16½ cm, 13½ cm, 15 cm, 17½ cm
The handles are ivory.
Marked: Hernstein & Son
Use: For incising and dissecting smaller more delicate tissue.

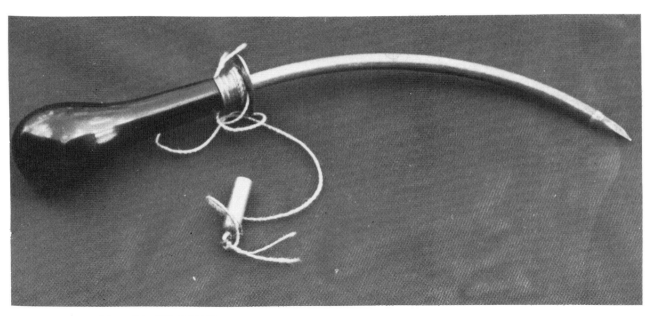

Illust. 24 TROCAR

Dimension: 21 cm
The handle is wooden.
Use: With its three-edged extremity, it is used to draw off various kinds of fluids, such as serum or pus.

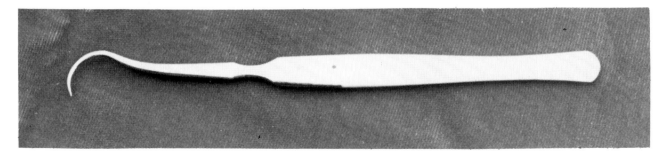

Illust. 25 TENACULUM

Dimensions: 16 cm
The handle is ivory.
Use: For pulling out the arteries from the stump in order to tie them off. Usually the silk suture material was placed around the instrument, and after the artery was extruded, the suture was slid from the instrument over the blood vessel and tied.

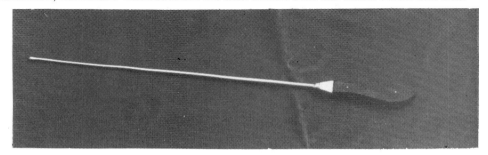

Illust. 26 FOREIGN BODY PROBE

Dimensions: 32cm
The handle is ebony.
Marked: W. Ford, N.Y.
Use: To locate foreign bodies in wound, either metal or bone. The end is blunt to avoid injury to arteries, vein, or nerve tissue.

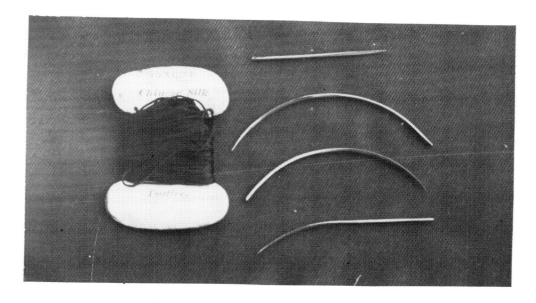

Illust. 27 SURGICAL SILK SUTURE MATERIAL (Left) and
ASSORTMENT OF SUTURE NEEDLES (Right)

Usually in a large surgical kit there were:
   12 surgeon's needles—6 straight and 6 curved
    6 wire suture needles—3 straight and 3 curved
   12 yards silver wire
   ¼ ounce silk
Use: To tie off major blood vessels and to close major defects in tissue.

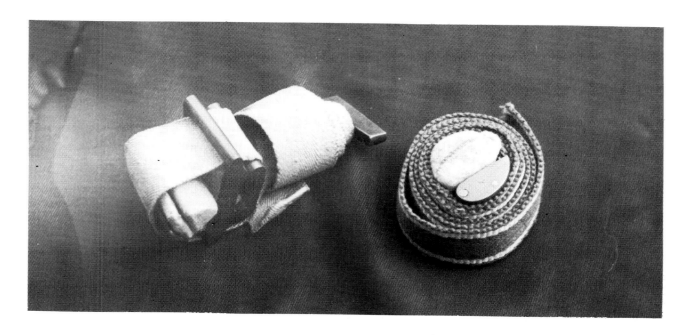

Illust. 28 TOURNIQUETS

On the left: Brass screw type
On the right: Belt buckle type
Uses: To reduce the amount of hemorrhage during surgical techniques. They put pressure on an artery, thereby limiting the amount of circulating blood in the area.

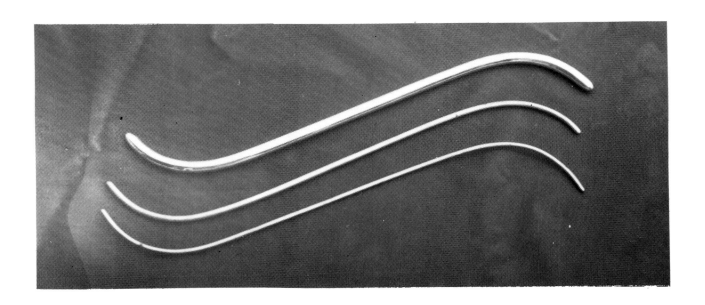

Illust. 29 STAVES OR SOUNDERS

Dimensions: 29 cm
Made of solid metal, German silver
Use: To locate calcific (stones) deposits in the urinary bladder. Also may be used
as urinary dilators.

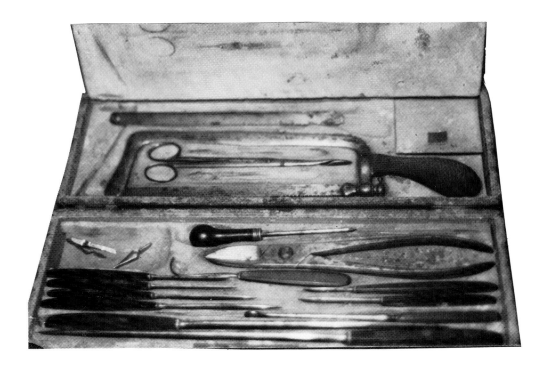

Illust. 30 CSA SURGICAL KIT

From the collection of Dr. Thomas Wheat.

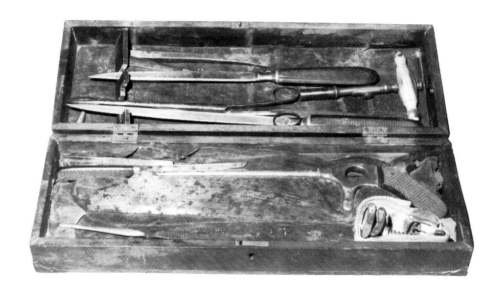

Illust. 31 LARGE STANDARD SIZED SURGEON'S KIT

This kit belonged to Surgeon James Miller, 30th Indiana Vol. Inf.
From the collection of James Brady, II.

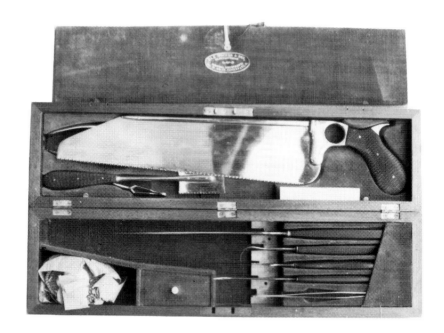

Illust. 32 LARGE AMPUTATION KIT

Marked: Max Wocher & Son
        Manufacturers
        Surgical Instruments
        105 W. 6th St.
        Cincinnati, O.
From the collection of Abraham Lincoln Memorial University Museum

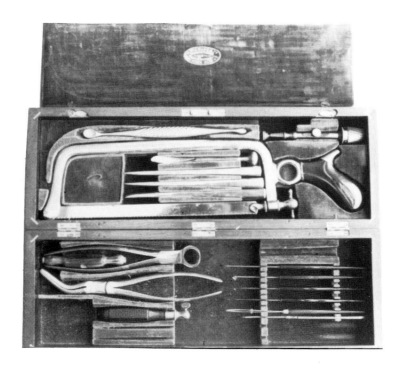

Illust. 33 LARGE SURGICAL AMPUTATING KIT
with Instruments for Resection

Marked: Tiemann & Co.
From the collection of Abraham Lincoln Memorial University Museum

Illust. 34 SURGEON'S CAPITAL OPERATING KIT (Opposite)
Photograph courtesy of Mutter Museum.

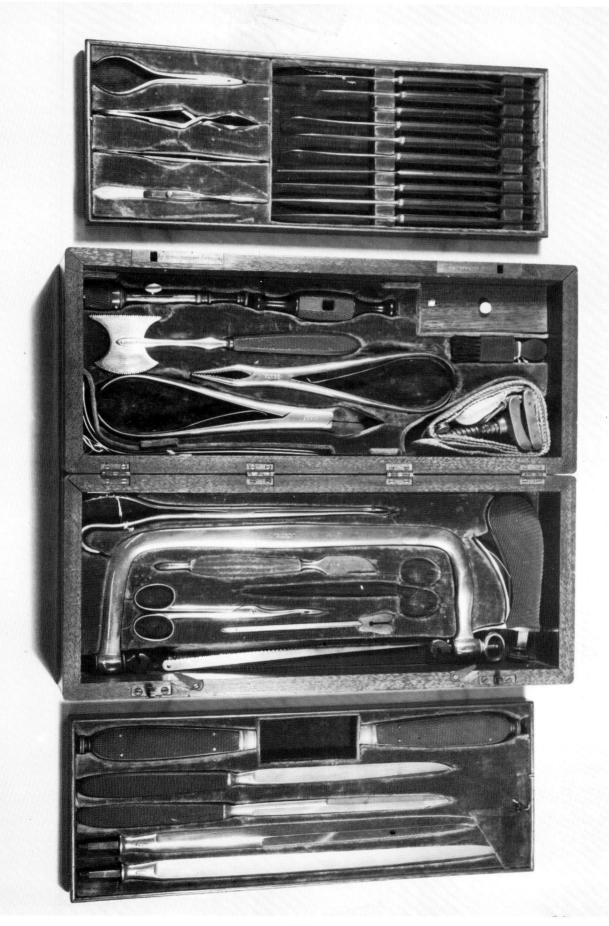

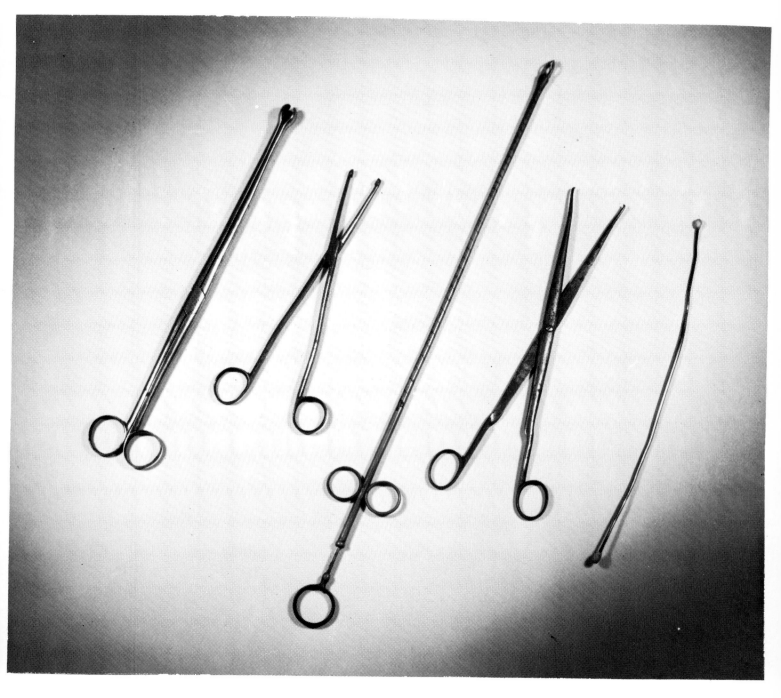

Illust. 36 BULLET FORCEPS

Left: forceps. Right: Nelaton's Probe.
The Nelaton's Probe is a piece of flexible wire with porcelain tip. It was used to detect lead bullets in wounds.
Photograph courtesy of Mutter Museum.

Illust. 35 OPERATING KIT (Opposite)

Marked: Shepard & Dudley
　　　　　　New York
Operating case and instruments were used in the years 1862, 1863, and 1864 by Dr. William West and Dr. John West of Illinois.
Photograph courtesy of Illinois State Historical Library.

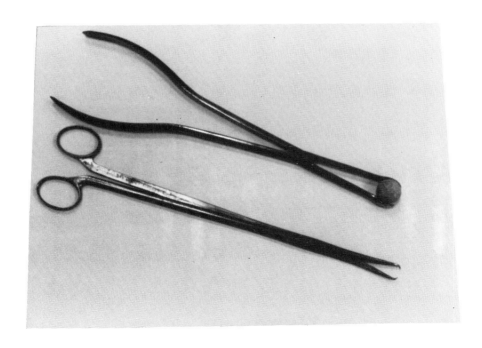

Illust. 37 BULLET FORCEPS
From the collection of Dr. Thomas Wheat.

Illust. 38 DIRECTOR
Dimensions: 11 cm in length.
Use: To position scalpel blade.

Illust. 39 FOREIGN BODY REMOVER
Dimensions: 12 cm in length.

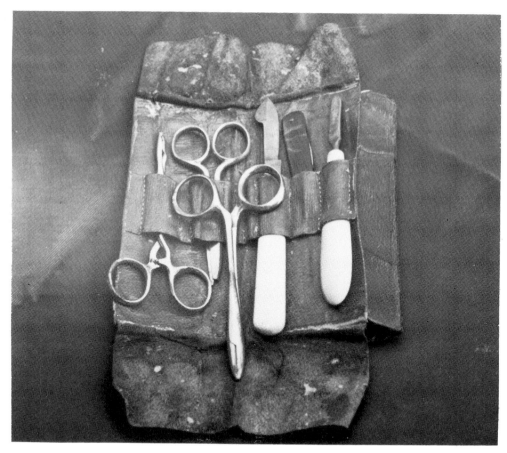

Illust. 40 POCKET OR ROLL UP
SURGICAL KIT

This kit was used during the Civil War.
The case is red leather and it contains
six instruments: two tissue forceps, one
scissors, two ivory handled scalpels,
and one tenaculum in tortoise shell case.

Illust. 41 SMALL LEATHER INSTRUMENT CASE

Dimensions: 12 cm×5 cm.
This case contains five instruments.

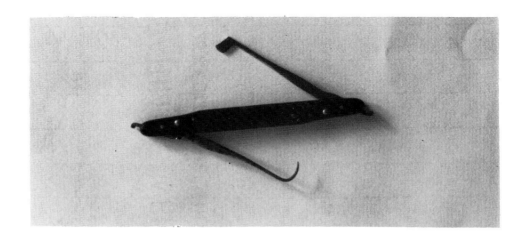

Illust. 42 COMBINATION TENACULUM AND LANCET

Holder is tortoise shell.
Dimension: 10 cm in length.

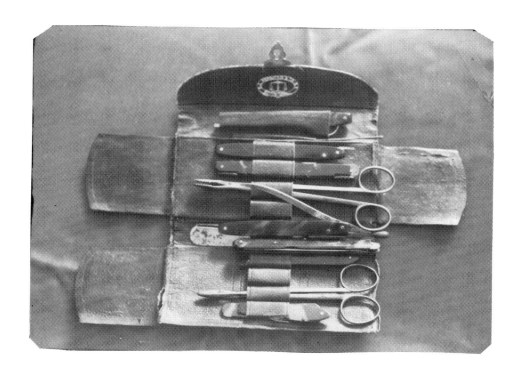

Illust. 43 POCKET SURGICAL KIT

The case is black leather. It contains 12 instruments, 7 of which have tortoise shell handles.
Marked: Hernstein & Co.
      N.Y.

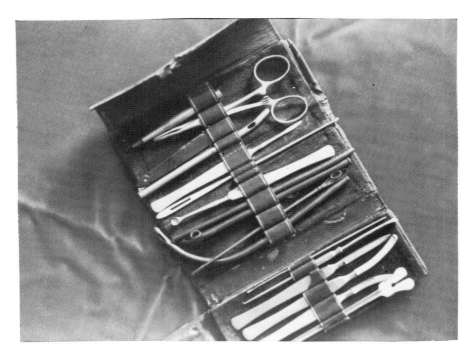

Illust. 44 POCKET SURGICAL KIT

Marked: Max Wocher & Son
           Surgical Instruments
           105 W. 6th St.
           Cincinnati, O.
This kit has a black leather case with purple silk lining. It contains 17 instruments.

Illust. 45 FOLDING SURGEON'S KIT

Made by Geo. Tiemann & Co.
Marked with makers name and "Dr. James Miller, Surgeon, U.S.A."
From the collection of James Brady, II.

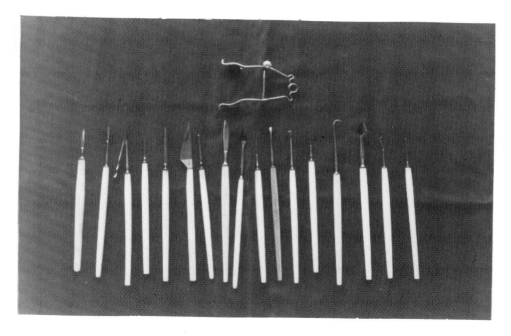

Illust. 46   INSTRUMENTS FOR EYE SURGERY

The handles are ivory.
Marked: Geo. Tiemann

Illust. 47   WOODEN HINGED BOX

Dimensions: 12.5 cm×5.5 cm×4.5 cm
Marked: Surgeon's Companion
The inside label reads: "Mitchell's Improved Adhesive Plaster. Pat. Feb. 3, 1863.
Manufactured by Novelty Plaster Works, Lowell, Mass. U.S.A."
This combination of isinglass plaster plus rubber was used for securing splints
on dislocated or broken limbs.

Illust. 48 WRAPPERS FOR FIELD TOURNIQUETS
The larger packaging contained one dozen individually wrapped tourniquets.

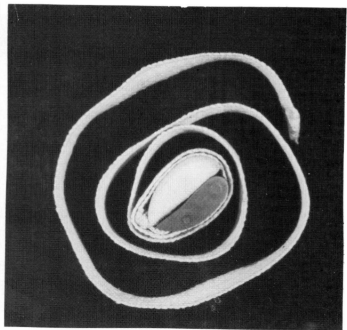

Illust. 49 FIELD TOURNIQUET —
BELT TYPE

Illust. 50 FIELD TOURNIQUET —
BELT BUCKLE TYPE

From the collection of James Brady, II.

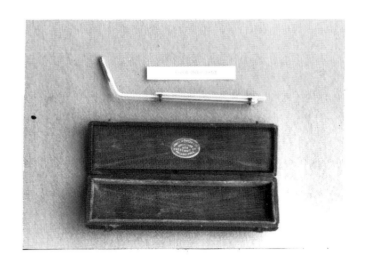

Illust. 51 EARLY INJECTING
SYRINGE

These syringes were beginning to be
used during the Civil War. Morphine, in
liquid form, was injected under the skin
to kill pain.

From the collection of Abraham Lincoln Memorial University Museum

Illust. 52 EARLY RECTAL
THERMOMETER

The thermometer was slowly being
introduced and used by the Medical
Profession during the Civil War. Not
many were used by Army or Navy Surgeons, however.

From the collection of Abraham Lincoln Memorial University Museum

Illust. 53 CIVIL WAR MEDICAL KNAPSACK

The outer covering is tarred canvas. The tin inserts contained medicines and the remaining space contained bandaging material. This was carried on the back of the Hospital Steward onto the battlefield.

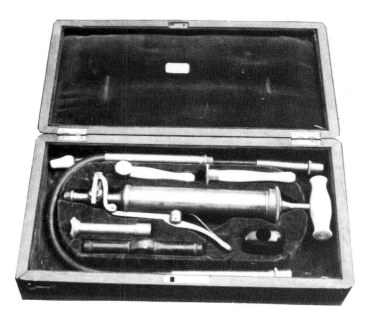

Illust. 54 STOMACH PUMP

Mahogany case with stomach pump apparatus. The case measures 27 cm × 14 cm × 5 cm.
Marked: John Wood
Manufacturer of Surgical Instruments
72 King St.
Manchester
The pump is made of brass and it has an ivory handle. The primary use was to eliminate poisonous material from the stomach and intestinal tract.

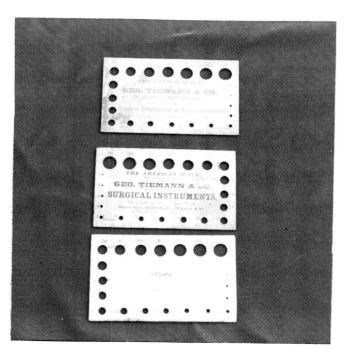

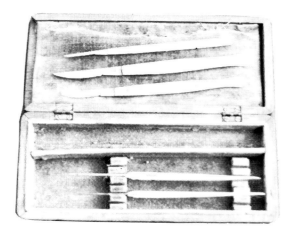

Illust. 55 URETHRAL INSTRUMENT SCALES

Marked: Geo. Tiemann & Co.
67 Chatam St.
New York
Top scale: The French scale is in c.m. (centimeters).
Middle scale: The American scale is in inches.
Bottom scale: This is an American scale made out of metal.
The top and middle scales are made out of cardboard.

Illust. 56 MAHOGANY INSTRUMENT CASE

The case contains five ivory-handled scalpels.
The case is 18 cm × 7½ cm × 2½ cm.
The lining is velvet.
These instruments were used for eye surgery, such as removal of cataracts.
The instruments' dimensions are: 12 cm, 14 cm, 13½ cm, 14½ cm, and 13½ cm.

Illust. 57 SURGEON'S BAG

This is a black leather bag with red interior. There is an eagle on the lock.
The dimensions are 24 cm × 17 cm × 11 cm.
Markings on the lock: Patent 1st out 1865
                            Neumann & Co.
It was probably used by surgeons to carry instruments and medicine.

Illust. 58 HYDROMETER WITH MAHOGANY CASE

The case measures 20 cm × 10 cm × 5 cm.
Marked: The lid of the case, inlaid in ivory, is marked with
            Sike's Hydrometer
            By Bate
            London
This kit dates from 1832. This instrument was used to compute the specific
gravity of liquids.

CHAPTER TWO

BLEEDING, VENISECTION SCARIFICATION & CUPPING

Before the Civil War, in the 1700s and early 1800s, medical knowledge adhered to the theory that inflammation and disease was caused by "tainted blood" or "bad blood." Their reasoning was that if you look at an area of inflammation you would see a red area swollen with blood. Present-day knowledge tells us that this happens because the body brings excess blood to fight infection. An increase of circulating white cells helps cure the disease.

Medical knowledge of the 1850s and 1860s held the opposite belief. It was felt there was an overabundance of blood (which was considered tainted) that had to be eliminated. The physicians would cut into the affected area and let the blood flow. This was called "bleeding" or "venisection,"

Illust. 59 to 67 show the various instruments used for this practice. The fleams actually opened into the veins, where the scarificator made many scratches into the skin and caused the bleeding. Today we know that these procedures only weakened the patient further and lessened hope for recovery. This knowledge was yet to be had in the 1800s.

Cupping devices are shown in Illust. 68. A cupping device introduced a counter-irritant to offset the pain caused by the disease. It was most frequently used on patients with pneumonia. The cup was filled with alcohol. The alcohol was ignited and the cup was pressed against the skin. A blister would be raised and then it was lanced. This procedure was believed to lessen the lung pain! It cured absolutely nothing. Some cups used a vacuum technique to raise the blister. Refer to Illust. 68. We should consider ourselves lucky that these practices ended in the 1880s.

Illust. 59 POCKET SURGICAL KIT

This kit contains three tortoise shell handled instruments:
Left instrument: Blunt-nosed scalpel.
Middle instrument: Pointed scalpel.
Right instrument: Hatchet scalpel used for lancing boils.
The case is made of black leather.

Illust. 60 SCARIFICATOR

The instrument measures: 4½ cm × 4½ cm
The case measures: 7 cm × 6 cm × 5 cm
Marked: J.B. Leitzel, M.D.
          Belvidere, Ill.
There are ten blades which protrude and are retracted by a spring mechanism.
These instruments were used for bleeding purposes and also for the introduction
of certain "medicines" into the body.

Illust. 61 SCARIFICATOR

Dimensions: 3.5 cm × 3.5 cm
There are 16 blades which retract with
a spring mechanism.
From the collection of Dr. Mark D.
Griffith.

Illust. 62 CASED SPRING
ACTIVATED BLEEDING DEVICE

From the collection of Dr. Thomas
Wheat.

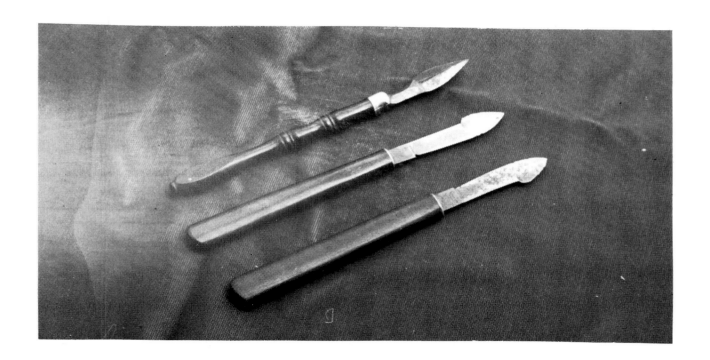

Illust. 63 VENISECTION KNIVES

Top knife: 15½ cm in length with an ebony handle.
Middle knife: 16 cm in length with an ebony handle.
Bottom knife: 15½ cm in length with an ebony handle.

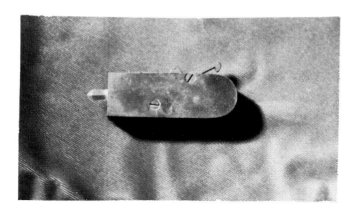

Illust. 64 FLEAM — SPRING ACTION

Dimensions: 7.5 cm × 2.5 cm.
Made of brass.
The action of this particular fleam is due to a spring device encased within the body of the instrument. The knife point would be drawn into the body of the instrument, then a trigger was pressed and the knife would thrust out and into the vein.

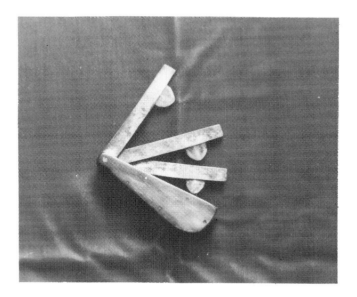

Illust. 65 TORTOISE SHELL HANDLED, THREE BLADE FLEAM

No markings.
When closed, it measures 8 cm.

Illust. 66 FLEAM WITH CARRYING CASE

Fleam dimensions: 8½ cm in length with brass sheath.
Case dimensions: 12 cm in length and made of pressed paper.

Illust. 67 SCARIFICATOR

Dimensions: 25½ cm in length
Marked: Mazdaznan

Illust. 68 EXAMPLES OF "CUPPING DEVICES" (Opposite)

Courtesy of the Armed Forces Institute of Pathology, Walter Reed Army
Medical Center

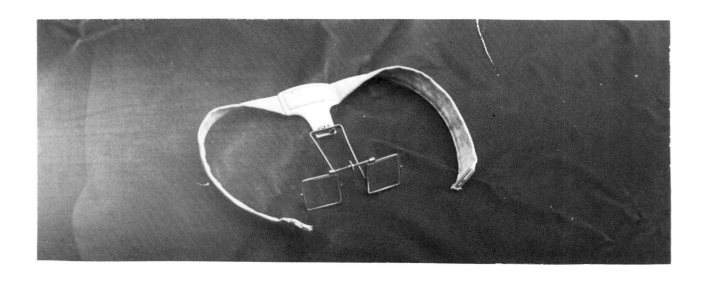

Illust. 69 MAGNIFYING GLASSES OR "LOUPES"

These were used by surgeons for detailed dissections. The head-band is cloth with an ivory front piece.

Illust. 70 DENTAL INSTRUMENTS

The leather case contains six dental instruments with ivory handles. These instruments were used for alveoplasty or bone reconstruction.
Case dimensions: 8.5 cm×6 cm
Instrument dimensions: 5.5 cm in length

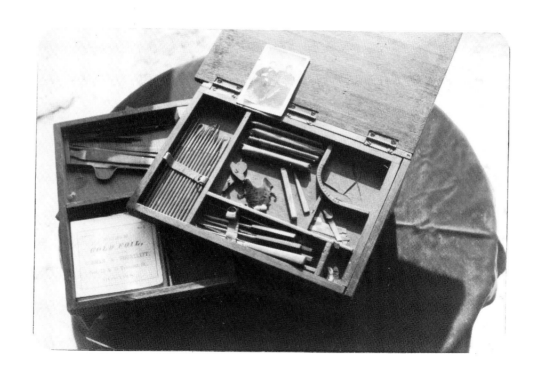

Illust. 71 PORTABLE DENTAL KIT
This kit was used during the Civil War.

CHAPTER THREE

❧

EMBALMING

It is because of the Civil War that the profession of mortuary science became prevalent. The requests of families to have the bodies of their loved ones transported home for proper memorial services made it necessary for a system of preservation to become a new profession.

The Physician's Pocket Memorandum published in 1869 by C.H. Cleveland, M.D., describes the way bodies were preserved in the 1860s. "A strong solution of the chloride of zinc—½ ounce of the salt to a quart of alcohol and water may be employed directly into the artery to prevent decomposition. Creosote is sometimes used as an anti-putrefactive agent, but its odor is objectionable...With a common pewter syringe, it may be thrown into the arterial system, the nozzle of the instrument being introduced into a slit made in the femoral artery.

"It is customary to transport bodies in metallic burial cases, or heavy wooden boxes lined with zinc plates."

Before the war there was no need for this type of service. Public pressure demanded the ascendancy of the profession of mortuary science.

***Illust. 72* CIVIL WAR ERA EMBALMING PUMP**

Case dimensions: 24 cm × 11 cm × 7 cm. It is made of wood and covered with leather. It is black in color and lined with green velvet.
The pump is 21.5 cm in length and 6.5 cm in diameter. The top is made of brass and the plunger knob is ivory.
Marked: Drage, 6 Tower Royal
       London

***Illust. 73* GLASS BOTTLE CONTAINING EMBALMING FLUID**

Marked: Durfee
       Embalming Fluid C.
       Grand Rapids
       Mich.

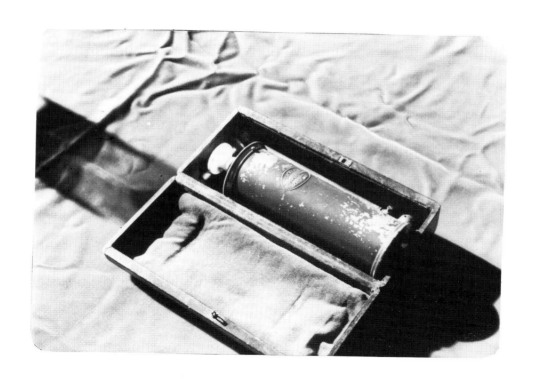

CHAPTER FOUR

THE WAR ON DISEASE

Of the 618,000 fatalities on both sides during the Civil War, about two-thirds (414,000) were the result of disease. Canon and cavalry were no defense in the surgeons' fight against these enemies.

From the official records of the Union Army we have the listing of the different diseases along with the number of deaths.

Cases	Disease	Deaths
75,368	Typhoid	27,050
2,501	Typhus	850
11,898	Continual Fever	147
49,871	Typho-malarial Fever	4,059
1,155,266	Acute diarrhea	2,923
170,488	Chronic diarrhea	27,558
233,812	Acute dysentery	4,084
25,670	Chronic dysentery	3,229
73,382	Syphillis	123
95,833	Gonorrhea	6
30,714	Scurvy	383
3,744	Delirium Tremens	450
2,410	Insanity	80
2,837	Paralysis	231

Acute and chronic dysentery are sometimes called fluxes, and the eruptive fevers are the diseases of small pox, measles, and scarlet fever. Gangrene is not mentioned in the official records because it was not thought of as a disease but the result of the operation. We know now that hospital gangrene is a result of a unique organism and should have been classified with the diseases. Instead of malarial fevers the term swamp fever was used; they mean the same.

Nature's curative powers and a good diet were often more effective than the physician's healing art in the 19th century, a time when doctors often did not know the causes of many disorders and could only treat symptoms. The prevalent medical theory of this time was that when a person was sick, the body was full of "ill-humors," and to rid the patient of these products, purgatives were given. It was not until World War II with the advent of antibiotics (especially penicillin) that we learned how to cure disease.

Without the benefit of modern medicine, however, the doctors of this time fought disorders with limited knowledge and various drugs available to them. One of the major forms of drug therapy was the use of home remedies by soldiers. Most of these remedies are in the category of eclectic medicine, that is, plant derivatives used for curatives.

A great many physicians believed in eclectic medicine. Surgeon D.J. Roberts CSA recalled how he resorted to the "indigenous resources to be found in our hills and dales, fields and forests, mountains and valleys." There were probably at least three laboratories established for the preparation of indigenous drugs: one in Lincolnton, North Carolina; one at Macon, Georgia; and one west of the Mississippi River in which tinctures and extracts were manufactured to some extent. Dr. Robert R. Smith, Jr., treated dysentery at a Cairo, Illinois, hospital by combining a fluid ounce extracted from a red-bud tree with three fluid ounces of aromatic syrup of rhubarb (Illust. 121).

The supply table also listed other available supplies and the amounts in which they were dispensed during the war. Medicinal whiskey, the old standby, was issued in the amount of 2,430,785 quarts. Also used were 978,943 ounces of sweet spirit of nitre; 2,072,040 ounces of cinchona (quinine) products; 1,232 ounces of strychnine and 539,712 pounds of magnesium sulphite.

The most striking item in the catalogue of statistics is the notation that the total issue of opium preparations (including powdered opium, powdered opium with ipecac, tincture of opium, and camphorated tincture of opium) was a staggering 2,841,596 ounces. In addition 442,926 dozen opium pills were prescribed. (Illust. 79 and 105).

The medical literature of the time seems to indicate that opium was used in the treatment of almost every infirmity and condition. Writing in 1865, Surgeon Joseph Woodward offered the following treatment for diarrhea, one of the most common and disabling ailments among the troops during the war.

Woodward combined diet and drugs in his prescription: "Food in a liquid or semi-liquid form is especially desirable because it is more readily digested. Milk is an exceedingly useful article of diet in these cases....Rice in almost any form is an excellent article....Beef tea, oysters and soft boiled eggs may also be used where the delunity is great, if, after trial they are found not to irritate the bowels...Sulfate of copper may be given in pill in the dose of 1/12 or 1/8 of a grain every two hours. If combined with opium, minute doses of of the latter agent should be employed, 1/8 to 1/4 of a grain of opium being combined in each pill...of the mineral acids, aromatic sulphuric acid is the most available: 10 drops may be given in sweetened water 3 to 4 times daily. It may be combined with laudanum (a solution of opium in alcohol) in equal quantities. Hope's camphor mixture, which is composed of a fluid drachm of nitrous acid, 40 drops of laudanum and 8 ounces of water has been found very useful in the dose of a tablespoon every 2 hours."

These were the wonder drugs of the time: quinine, bromine, ether, chloroform, opium, and morphine derivatives. We have discussed ether and chloroform, and the pain killers, opium and morphine, in the surgical chapter. Now we turn our attention to bromine and quinine.

Bromine was the choice drug for hospital gangrene. This disease was the most prevalent killer of post-amputation patients. Medical knowledge of the 1860s attributed this disease to overcrowding, bad ventilation, and want of cleanliness. Also the scorbutic patient, or one with an enfeebled constitution was susceptible to the disease. Today we know that a particular baterium is the cause of gangrene. The reason for the spread of the disease during the Civil War was the lack of sterile conditions and instruments, to say nothing of the surgeons' hands themselves. This disease is highly contagious, and by using instruments and hands that were not sterile, the disease spread from patient to patient.

The use of bromine was a benefit to the soldier who had contracted gangrene. Dr. M. Goldsmith, surgeon U.S. Vol., gave this advice on the use of bromine: The patient should be rendered insensible by the use of anesthetic—chloroform or ether. The wound should be thoroughly cleaned with warm water and soap. The surface to be treated with bromine should be dried. This cleansing was done with a swab of lint. The pure bromine would be introduced with a small, glass pipette. The surrounding tissue would be swabbed to within one inch of the wound with a solution of bromine and water. Hospital gangrene was also treated with potassium permanganate, spirits of turpentine, and silver nitrate. All of these materials were caustic to the tissue and ate away the area of infection. In most cases they did not cure the patient but temporarily ridded him of the infection. In rare cases he might overcome the infection, survive the treatment and live.

For the treatment of miasmatic fever or malarial disease, the choice drug during the war was quinine. This alkaloid was prepared from various species of cinchona bark, which contained a combination of kinic acid and the astringent principle called cinchotannic acid (Ilust. 78 and 80). The most common salt used during the Civil War was Quininae Sulphas, U.S.A. It is interesting to note that page 649 of "A Treatise on Pharmacy" written by Edward Parrish in 1864, mentions "that Dr. Pepper and other practitioners connected with hospital practice have used sulphate of quinidia in the same or less doses than the salt of quininia..." Could this be the Dr. Pepper for whom a popular soft drink is named?

In 1862 the Sanitary Commission published a report on Quinine. It states, "...Now it is a well established fact in the experience of American physicians, that the daily use of a small quantity of quinine, say from three to six grains, in one or more doses, by those who are exposed to the danger of malarial poisoning, will in most instances prevent an attack of malarial disease, and that it will always render the disease milder, if it should occur. It will also prevent the development of malarial cachexia."

It is interesting to follow the process by which Quiniae Sulphus was prepared during the war. "It is in feathery white crystals much interlaced; of its eight equivalents of water, six are given off by exposure to dry air, while the remaining two are driven off at 248 degrees. It dissolves in 740 parts of cold and 30 parts of hot water, in 60 parts of alcohol, but scarcely in ether. The addition of a mineral or of certain organic acids renders it easily soluable."

After dealing with the wonder drugs we should mention the most controversial preparation of that period. Calomel was the drug that cost Surgeon General Hammond his job. The chief ingredient in calomel was the element mercury. Calomel is prepared by boiling sulphuric acid on mercury. This procedure forms the presulphate. This mixture is then heated with a common salt which in turn forms chloride of mercury and sulphate of soda. This combination is a very powerful irritant when taken in large doses. It causes burning of the epigastrium, vomiting and purging. When it is applied to the skin, it is corrosive. Today we know that any mercury compound is a deadly poison and not to be used internally. Hammond could foresee this problem and issued circular #6 which banned calomel from the Army Supply Table. This order enraged the older surgeons (vintage the War of 1812), and they plotted to have Hammond removed. In November of 1863 false charges "relating to liquor contracts" were brought against Hammond while he was conveniently away on business. As a consequence of the Surgeon General's demand for satisfaction, a kangaroo trial was held. Hammond was formally charged and found guilty of conduct unbecoming an officer and a gentleman. He was dismissed from the Service in August of 1864. A dozen years after the War, the case was reviewed and the hand of justice restored Hammond, then an outstanding neurosurgeon, to the rank of brigadier general.

Calomel continued to be used during the War, but its use was on the decline. This decline was good news for the ill soldier. Mercury compounds in an ointment form were used until World War II for the treatment of syphilis.

In conclusion, let us list the contents of the U.S. Army Medicine Pannier:

1. Cantharides
2. Silver Nitrate
3. Silver Chloride
4. Iodine
5. Tartar Emetic (Illust. 106)
6. Mecurous Chloride (Calomel) (Illust. 107)
7. Beef Extract
8. Coffee Extract
9. Condensed Milk
10. Alcohol
11. Black Tea
12. Spirit of nitrous ether
13. Strong Alcohol
14. Cough mixture
15. White sugar
16. Chloroform (Illust.111)
17. Liniment
18. Syrup of squill (Illust. 113)
19. Ammonia water
20. Ether (Illust. 91)
21. Opium (Illust. 112)
22. Fluid extract of cinchona
23. Fluid extract of valerian
24. Fluid extract of ginger (Illust. 114)
25. Olive oil
26. Oil of turpentine
27. Glycerine
28. Paragoric
29. Ferric Sulphate
30. Spirits of ammonia
31. Cathartic pills (Illust. 112)
32. Ipecac pills
33. Ipecac powder
34. Quinine sulphate (Illust. 102)
35. Potassium chlorate
36. Potassium bicarbonate (Illust. 117)
37. Potassium iodine
38. Rochelle salt
39. Morphine
40. Camphor & opium pills
41. Mercury pills
42. Opium pills
43. Tannic acid
44. Alum (Illust. 126)
45. Callodion
46. Creasote (Illust. 90)
47. Fluid extract of aconite
48. Fluid extract of colchicine
50. Tincture of ferric chloride
51. Lead acetate (Illust. 120)
52. Zinc sulphate

This list was the supply of ammunition from which the Civil War surgeon drew to defend his patients from the ravages of disease. There was not much in the way of curative powers in any of these compounds. The best line of defense was to stay healthy; the odds of that occurring were staggering. We can look back and poke fun at the healers of the 1860s, but who knows what will be said in the distant future about the medicine of the 1980s?

Illust. 74 MEDICAL SADDLE BAGS (Opposite)

Bags were used by physicians before, during and after the Civil War.
Each bag is 22 cm × 21 cm × 10 cm and has top compartment plus small pouch and the pull out drawer containing 17 glass vials (9 in one and 8 in the other).
Each vial is 10 cm × 2½ cm, the contents still in some of the vials are as follows:
Hyd. Chlo. Mit

Pulv. Dover Opium and Ipecacuania	Treatment of Diarrhea
2 Zinci. Sulph.	Astringent
Pulv. Opii.	Narcotic (pain killer)
Pulv. Rhei. - Rhubarb	Laxative
Potass. Chloras	
Pulv. Aloes	Laxative or Carhartic
2 Ipecac	Treat. of Diarrhea and dys.
Potass. Iodine	
Ferric Compound	Tonics and Astringent
Not marked	
4 Empty	

The top compartment most probably carried bandage material, apothecary equipment and measuring devices.

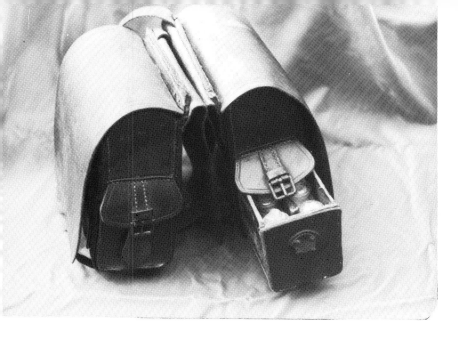

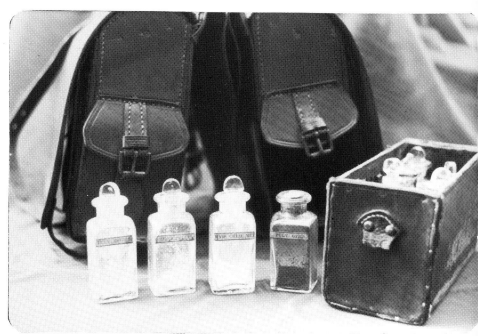

Illust. 75 MEDICAL SADDLE BAGS
Containing original glass vials. Black leather.
From the collection of the Lincoln Memorial University Museum.

Illust. 76 U.S. ARMY MEDICAL CASE for field service
31 cm×17 cm×15 cm. Black leather.

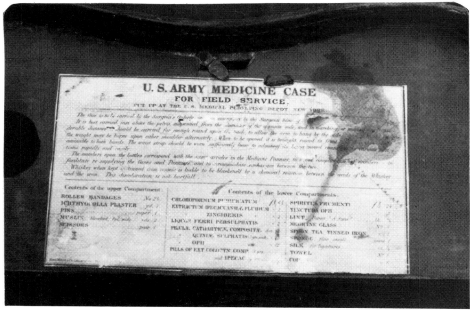

Illust. 76a and 76b TABLE OF CONTENTS OF FIELD MEDICAL CASE

24 Roller Bandages
1 yd. Ichthyocolla Plaster
1 paper of pins
2 yds. Bleached Muslin
1 paid Scissors

Chloroform
Ipecac Extract
Zinc Sulphate
Ferric Sulphate
Quinine Sulphate
Opii
Pills of Colocyn Comp. 3 grs.
Pills of Ipecac ½ grs.

UPPER COMPARTMENT
Use primarily for wound bandaging

Spirits Fermenti
Opii Tincture
Lint
Medicine Glass
Teaspoon   Tinned Iron
Sponge
Silk (Suture)
Towel

This case was put up by the U.S. Medical Purveying Depot, New York. It was to be carried by the surgical orderly or in an emergency by the surgeon himself. It was carried suspended by the shoulder and supported by a waist strap. "Whiskey when kept in tinned iron vessels is liable to be blackened by a chemical reaction between the acids of the whiskey and the iron. This discoloration is *not* hurtfull." (quote from directions)

Illust. 77

Some of the tinned iron medicine containers found in the Field Medical Case.
Tin marked Quinine Sulphate is 10.5 cm×5 cm×5 cm.
The smaller tin marked Quinine is 8.5 cm×3.5 cm×3.5 cm.
All have cork stoppers except the large one on the left (top picture). It has a
screw top and measures 12.5 cm×6 cm×6 cm.

Illust. 78 TIN MEDICAL
CONTAINER

8 cm. ×3.5 cm ×3.5 cm.
Contents: Pillae Quiniae Sulphatis.
Each pill is 3 grs. Prepared at U.S.A.
Med. Purveying Depot, Astoria, L.I.

Illust. 79 TIN MEDICINE
CONTAINER

10½ cm in height. The remnants of the
label read: "Pulvis...Opii"
Also the label has the remains of the
label of the Astoria, L.I., Medical
Purveying Depot.

Illust. 80 MEDICAL TIN
CONTAINER

10 cm ×5 cm ×5 cm.
Contents: Pills of Quiniae Sulph. 4 gr.
Prepared at U.S.A. Laboratory,
Philadelphia.

Illust. 81 FIELD MEDICAL CHEST

Used by Surgeon George King of the 16th Regt. Mass. Inf.
From the collection of Dr. Thomas Wheat.

Illust. 82
Medicine Chest used by Surgeon William H. King of the 149th Pennsylvania
Infantry.
Chest is 21 cm×15 cm and covered with black leather.

Illust. 83 MEDICINE CHEST CONTAINING ORIGINAL GLASS VIALS

Wooden box covered with leather. 19½"×8½"×6½" in dimensions. From the collection of Lincoln Memorial University Museum.

Illust. 84 SMALL MEDICINE KIT WITH ORIGINAL GLASS VIALS

From the collection of Lincoln Memorial University Museum.

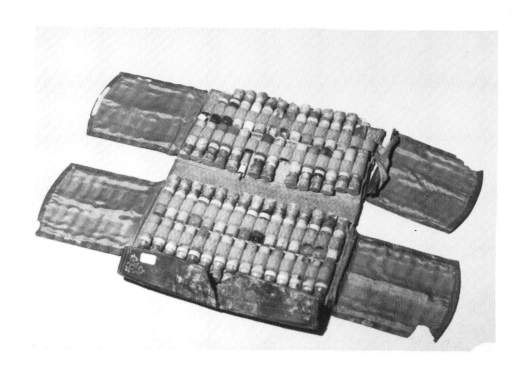

Illust. 85 MEDICINE KIT

Contains small glass vials with contents still inside. Kit was patented in 1861. From the collection of James Brady, II.

Illust. 86
Leather container for 10 glass medicine vials. 145 cm×9 cm×3 cm. Vials are 13 cm long and have cork stoppers.
The vials were marked but have been obliterated except for one which is marked Castor Oil.

Illust. 87 SMALL MEDICINE KIT
Three glass vials. Case is black leather.
Marked 5th N.Y.V.
From the collection of Lincoln Memorial University Museum.

Illust. 88 CLEAR GLASS HOSPITAL BOTTLE

Dimensions: 23 cm in height, 8.5 cm in diameter.
Marked: South Carolina Dispensary with Palmetto Tree.

Illust. 89 AMBER COLORED HOSPITAL BOTTLE

Dimensions: 23.5 cm in height, 8.5 cm in diameter.
Marked: USA HOSP DEPT
The "Red Glass" bottle was used to keep mercury, silver nitrate and also chloroform—used as an anesthetic.

Illust. 90 GLASS BOTTLE (12.5 cm)

Marked USA Medical Dept. put up at
the U.S.A. Laboratory, Philadelphia,
Pa., 1863.
2 oz. Creasotum.
The principal use of creasote internally
is to check nausea. For this purpose
about two drops may be dissolved in
water (1 oz.) and a little gum and sugar
added.
Solution was dropped upon a fragment
of cotton. After dilution with Alcohol,
Ether or Chloroform, it was inserted into the cavity of a tooth to relieve a
toothache.

Illust. 91 TIN CONTAINER
FOR ETHER

Dimensions: 12.5 cm high and 9 cm
in diameter.
Label reads: Stronger Ether for
Anesthetic. Prepared by Edward P.
Squibb, M.D., Brooklyn, N.Y.

Illust. 92   MEDICINE MINIE BALL

Dimensions: 1.7 cm in diameter.
This is a round musket ball that was used by soldiers during a time of surgery or intense pain. The lead projectile would be placed between the patient's teeth and the patient would be instructed to bite hard during a painful procedure.
Care should be given to identify the marks of human teeth bites because sometimes swine would root these up and the marks produced are those of the swine.

Illust. 93   LARGE GLASS STOPPERED BOTTLE

Light green in color. 27 cm in height. 9 cm in diameter.

Illust. 94   GLASS APOTHECARY CONTAINERS

26 cm high. 8.5 cm in diameter.
These would be found primarily in apothecary shops and not as part of the Army's issue. The container marked Lin. Camph. Co. is marked on the bottom with W.N. Walton. Pat. Sept. 23, 1862. The container marked Tinct. Arnigae is marked in the same way.

Illust. 95 FLUTED PRESCRIPTION VIAL

Light green in color and 13 cm high.

Illust. 96 CLEAR GLASS MEDICINE BOTTLE WITH GLASS STOPPER

Dimensions: 11 cm high and 4.5 cm in diameter at the base.

Illust. 97 MEDICINE FLASK

The glass is clear and it has a pewter removable bottom plus a pewter screw cap. 20 cm high.

Illust. 98 GINGER BEER BOTTLE

Dimensions: 20.5 cm in length and 7.5 cm in diameter at its base.
Top color is brown, bottom 2/3 is tan earthenware material. It is unmarked.

Recipe for Ginger Beer:
Race Ginger (bruised) 4 oz.
Bitartrate of potassa 3 oz.

Mix these and add 5 lbs. of sugar loaf, 2 lemons and 5 gal. of water. Let stand 12 hrs. then add teacup of yeast. Bottle immediately and securely.

Illust. 99 OFFICER'S WHISKEY
FLASK
Belonging to Surgeon W.H. Wilbur, 1st
Brigade, 2nd Cavalry Division.
Dimensions: 15.5 cm high.
Leather covered with pewter bottom.

Illust. 100
Standard Infantry canteen that was
used by Medical Dept. for dispensing
Quinine. 19 cm with cork stopper and
cloth shoulder strap.

Illust. 101
Oval or "kidney bean" medical canteen. Marked U.S. M. Dept. The canteen is
24 cm×16.5 cm, and has a brass screw stopper.

Illust. 102   PAPER CONTAINER OF QUININE

Dimensions: 6 cm in diameter, 2 cm deep.
Label reads: S.H. Williams & Co.
　　　　　Druggists
　　　　　Quinine
　　　　　183 Shelton Ave.
　　　　　New ...
These are crystals of quinine to be mixed or dissolved in water or alcohol.

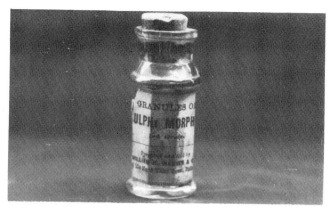

Illust. 103   GLASS MEDICINE BOTTLE CONTAINING MORPHIAE SULPHAS

Dimensions: 7 cm in length×2.5 cm in diameter.
Label reads: Granules of
　　　　　Sulph: Morphia
　　　　　1-4 grains
　　　　　Prepared by
　　　　　WM. R. Warner & Co.
　　　　　154 No. Third St.
　　　　　Phila.
This is a white feathery crystal of morphine. Soluble in two parts of hot water. Most common morphine sold in the U.S. at the time of the Civil War.

Illust. 104   MEDICINE GLASS BOTTLE

Dimensions: 4.5 cm in diameter. 8 cm deep.
Marked: JUGLANDIN
　　　　　H.M. MERRELL & CO.
　　　　　Manufacturine Chemists
　　　　　Cincinnati
Juglandin is a laxative, diuretic, and in larger doses a cathartic agent. It is prepared from the bark of the root of Juglans Cineria, Butternut or White Walnut.

Illust. 105 GLASS VIAL WITH OPIUM PILLS

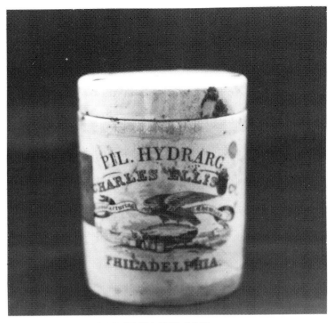

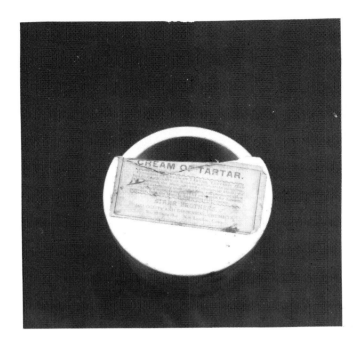

Illust. 106 APOTHECARY JAR

Dimensions: 7½ cm in diameter × 10 cm deep.
Made of porcelain.
Imprinted in blue lettering is:

PIL. HYDRARG

Charles Ellis & Co. Philadelphia

with picture of an eagle

PIL. HYDRARG is Pilulae Hydrargyri, U.S.P. commonly known as "Blue mass." This is a mixture of mercury, powdered liquorice, powdered rose leaves and honey. A paper label of Cream of Tartar has been affixed to the jar. Cream of Tartar is potassae of bitartas. This label was probably affixed later.

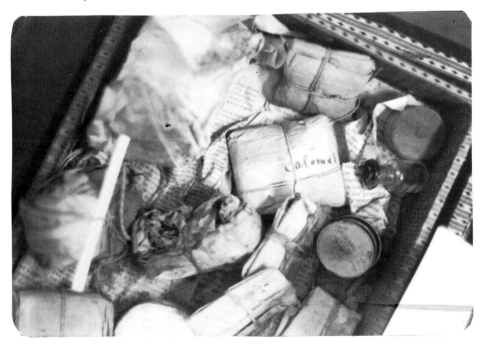

Illust. 107

Packaged Calomel "Deadly mecurial compound." This was also labeled "Blue mass." Contained in a C.S.A. surgeon's kit.
From the collection of Lincoln Memorial University Museum.

Illust. 108
Medicine vial made of wood. 6.5 cm high and 2 cm in diameter. Label reads: J.F. Hadley, M.D.

Illust. 109 HOSPITAL DRUG CHEST

This is a mahogany chest which measures 73 cm×36 cm×48 cm. It contains 48 medicine containers. Each container, which is made of glass or porcelain, contains a different compound or mixture used to treat disease during the Civil War.

Illust. 110

2 oz. glass graduate found in the Hospital Drug Chest.

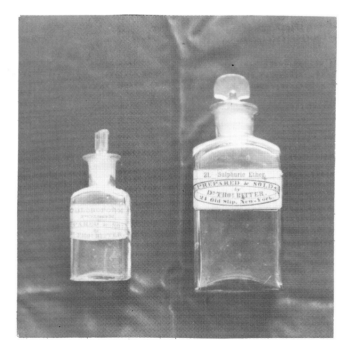

Illust. 111

Glass vials containing ether and chloroform which were used as anesthetics during the Civil War.

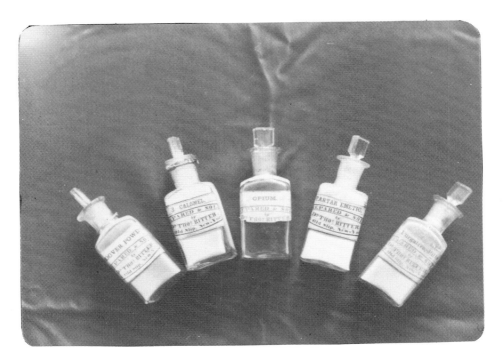

Illust. 112

Glass vials containing the most common "medicines" of the Civil War. Dover's Powder, Calomel, Tartar Emetic and Purgative Pills were used to ride the body of "ill humors."

Illust. 113 **VIAL OF SYRUP OF SQUILLS**

Glass vial containing Syrup of Squills. This syrup is made the following way: Take coarse powder of Squill, mix 4 troyounces of Seneka, with 48 grains of Tartrate of Antimony and Potassium and 42 troyounces of sugar. This is mixed with dilute Alcohol and water. This syrup was used as a remedy for pulmonary affections—harassing coughs.

Illust. 114 **GLASS BOTTLE CONTAINING TINCT. OF GINGER**

Tincture of Ginger is a mixture of ginger and alcohol. It is also known as Zingiber. It was used as a rubefacient on the skin.

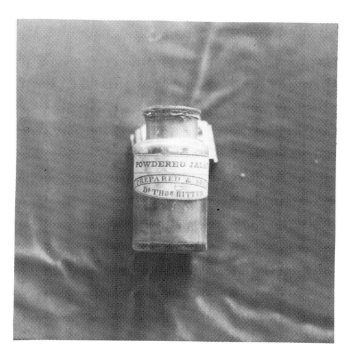

Illust. 115 GLASS CONTAINER
FOR POWDERED SASSAFRAS

It was used as a mild stimulant diaphoretic. A diaphoretic is a medicine that
increases the function of perspiration or
lowering body temperature.

Illust. 116 GLASS CONTAINER
FOR POWDERED JALAP

It is obtained from the root of the Jalap
plant and is used as a cathartic and a
nauseant.

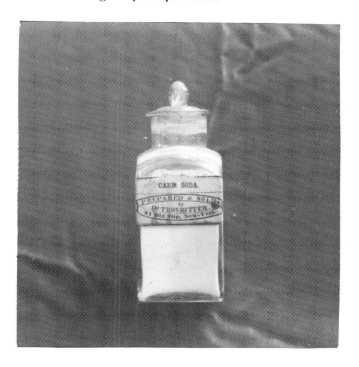

Illust. 118 GLASS CONTAINER
FOR SPIRITS OF TURPENTINE

Turpentine, which comes from the pine
tree, was used to treat chronic rheuma-
tism, chronic bronchitis and also as a
diuretic. It was also used as an athel-
mintic—which destroyed or expelled
worms from the intestine.

Illust. 117: GLASS CONTAINER FOR
CARBONATE OF SODA

The chief use then was as now as an
antacid.

Illust. 119 GLASS CONTAINER FOR CALCINED MAGNESIA

It was used for excessive flatulence with acidity of the stomach. The usual dose was one teaspoon every 4 hours.

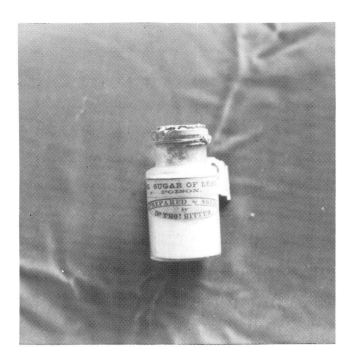

Illust. 120 GLASS CONTAINER FOR SUGAR OF LEAD

This was a mineral astringent for internal hemorrhage from dysentery.

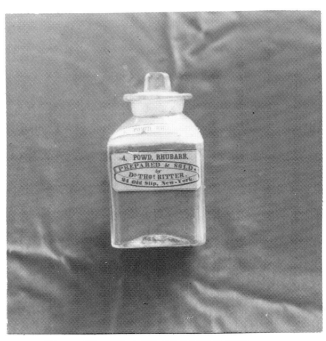

Illust. 121 GLASS CONTAINER FOR POWDERED RHUBARD

Rhubarb was mixed with water or alcohol and used as a cathartic and a laxative. The dose as a laxative would be 5 to 10 grains; as a purgative it would be 20 to 30 grains.

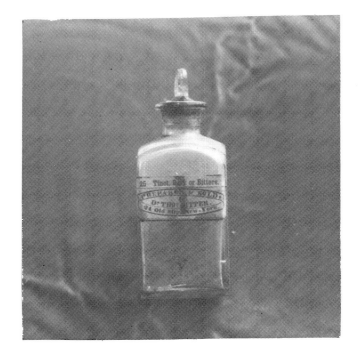

Illust. 122 GLASS CONTAINER FOR BITTERS

Simple bitters increased the appetite and promoted digestion. Most, if not all, were derived from plants or barks.

Illust. 123 GLASS CONTAINER FOR A SULPHUR AND IRON MIXTURE

This was prepared by dissolving iron wire in diluted sulphonic acid. This was used as a wound disinfectant.

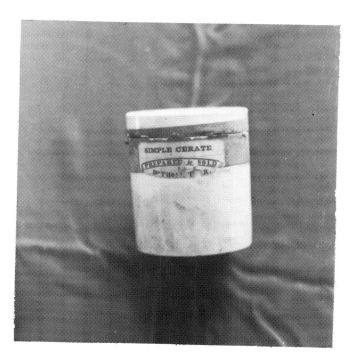

Illust. 124 PORCELAIN JAR CONTAINING SIMPLE CERATE

This is a healing agent applied to the skin. Cerates were usually made from bland fats and fixed oils.

Illust. 125 PORCELAIN JAR CONTAINING BLISTERING PLASTER

This was a "medicine" when applied to the skin produced a blister. They were a "stimulant" to the system. One common one was known as "Spanish Fly."

Illust. 126 LARGE PORCELAIN JAR CONTAINING POWDERED ALUM

Alum is a powdered astringent, used both externally and internally.

Illust. 127 LARGE PORCELAIN JAR CONTAINING EPSOM SALTS

It was used as a saline cathartic. Because of its bitter taste it was mixed with coffee or lemon juice.

Illust. 128 LARGE PORCELAIN JAR CONTAINING SULPHUR

Sulphur was used during the Civil War as a mineral cathartic.

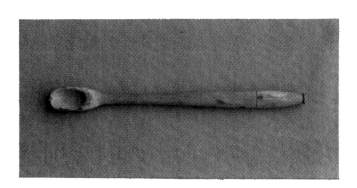

Illust. 129 WOODEN SPOON USED FOR APOTHECARY OR DRUG USE

Illust. 130 PORCELAIN PHARMACY FUNNEL AND FILTER

Dimensions: 10.5 cm in diameter. The funnel was also called a tunnel and was used to direct liquids into a specific place. It also was used with a filter paper to produce a liquid filter system.

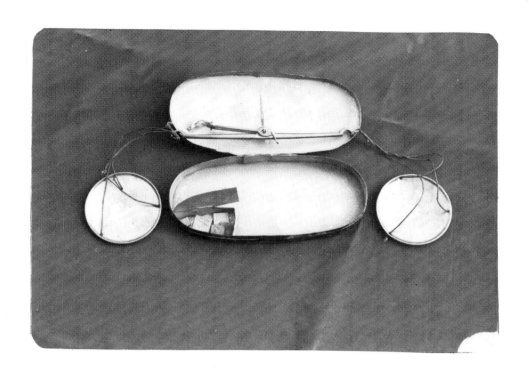

Illust. 131 **PRESCRIPTION SCALES WITH JAPANNED TIN CASE**
Case is 16 cm×7.5 cm×2.5 cm. There is an eagle painted on the cover, inside is
orange in color. The scales are brass with steel struts.

Illust. 132 EARTHENWARE
MORTAR & PESTLE MARKED
WEDGEWOOD

Mortar is 11.5 cm in diameter and 7 cm
in height.
Pestle is 20 cm in length.
The mortar and pestle were used to
grind solids into fine powders to be used
in medicines.

Illust. 133 MORTAR AND PESTLE
MADE OF BRASS

Mortar is 10.5 cm in diameter and 7.5
cm deep.
Pestle is 18 cm in length.
There are no markings on either the
mortar or pestle.

Illust. 134 LARGE SIZE EARTHENWARE MORTAR AND PESTLE

Mortar is 23 cm in diameter and 14 cm deep.
Pestle is 30 cm in length.
The wooden handle is stamped with US 1861.

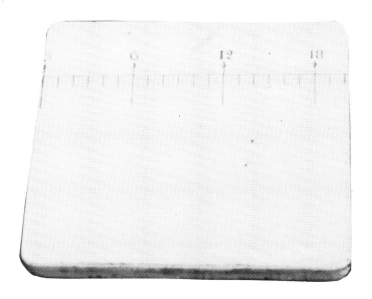

Illust. 135 GRADUATED PILL TILE

Dimensions: 12.5 cm × 12.5 cm.
The pill tile was made of porcelain or queensware and was useful in preparing certain ointments and pills. Tiles were made in various sizes and sometimes graduated, as seen above, to facilitate the division of masses into 12 or 24 pills.

Illust. 136 GLASS MEASURING DEVICE FOR LIQUIDS AND CARRYING CASE

Case measures 6 cm × 6 cm in diameter. Glass is 5 cm diameter by 5.5 deep. Etched upon the glass are teaspoon and tablespoon graduations. The color of the case is green with gold lettering.

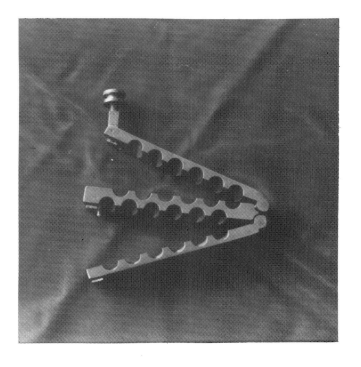

Illust. 137 BRASS SUPPOSITORY FORMER

Dimensions: 12 cm × 2.5 cm.
Marked: #4.

Illust. 138 MICROSCOPE

Civil War period microscope in mahogany case. Microscope is constructed of brass. It is 37 cm high and the box is 22 cm×15 cm×7.5 cm. The interior of the case contains the disassembled microscope and assorted apparatus for the mounting of glass slides.

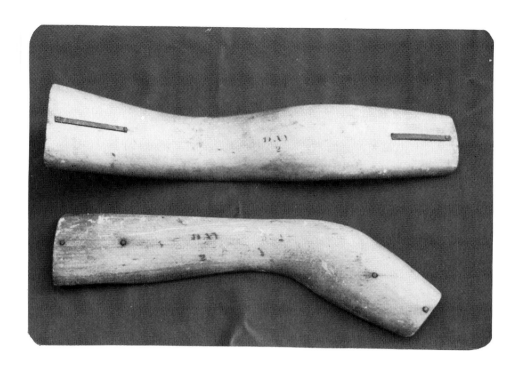

Illust. 139 WOODEN SPLINTS (Maple)

Patented by Almiron M. Day of Bennington, Vermont. The top leg splint was positioned behind the thigh and calf. It is 37 cm×8.5 cm. The bottom splint is an arm splint that was positioned on medial and lateral aspects of upper and lower arm. It is 37 cm×8.5 cm.

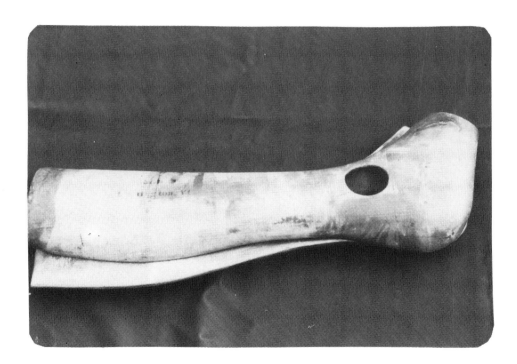

Illust. 139 WOODEN SPLINT — A.M. DAY, Bennington, Vt., 1853

It was used for the lower leg and ankle. It is 44 cm×12 cm.

Illust. 141 INVALID FEEDING SPOONS

Two pair of feeding spoons, one large and one small. Originally these spoons had large circular handles for easy grasping by the patients in Civil War hospitals.

Illust. 140 ARTIFICIAL LEG

This leg belonged to Pvt. Peleg Bradford, Jr. of the 1st Maine Heavy Artillery. Pvt. Bradford was wounded in 1864 at Petersburg.

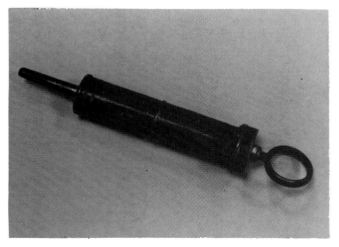

Illust. 142 PEWTER SYRINGE

Used to inject powders into ears and wounds. From the collection of Dr. Thomas Wheat.

Illust. 143 INVALID FEEDING CUP

Made of white porcelain. 7.5 cm high and 12 cm in diameter. This was used to feed broth and soups to hospital patients.

CHAPTER FIVE

MEDICAL INSIGNIA AND UNIFORMS

If you ever want to start a debate among Civil War medical collectors, start talking about the color green with respect to uniforms and insignia. Was green the branch designation or not? There is agreement that there was a green sash worn by surgeons of both the Union and Confederate Armies. (Illust. 149). There is also a uniform identified with a Union surgeon with a green velvet collar and green cuffs. (Illust. 145). To add further favorable evidence to the green theory, there is an example of an identified green sword knot. (Illust. 160).

The problem arises with the shoulder straps worn by the Union surgeons and assistant surgeons. Was there a green coloration to these? There never has been demonstrated such a strap. Illust. 152 shows the typical strap with the MS designation. The coloration is dark or midnight blue, which was the color of the Staff. To complicate this a bit, Illust. 144 shows an identified surgeon's uniform. This uniform, along with the sash, gauntlets, and sword, was used by Surgeon James Fitzpatrick of the 9th Mass. Vol. Inf. The shoulder straps that designate a rank of Captain have a green color. The buttons also indicate Infantry. The only reasoning for this uniform is that it was an interim one that he used during the time when he was an assistant surgeon until he became a Major and a full surgeon in charge of a hospital in Georgetown.

Illust. 146 and 147 depict the type of hat insignia worn by Union surgeons. Illust. 146 displays the slouch hat while Illust. 147 shows the kepie. In Illust. 156 we see the MS which stood for medical staff, while in Illust. 154 the US stood for staff officer. The insignia in Illust. 155 has the designation MD for medical department.

There is a theory that the MD insignia did not appear until after the Civil War but the medical department insignia, MD, is shown in many Civil War documents and equipment. That suggests that MS and MD were used interchangeably during the War between the States.

The Confederate medical officer's uniform shown in Illust. 150 is typical of that which a Confederate surgeon would wear. It is made of gray cloth with black piping. It also has an accompanying green sash. The pants would have been black with a gold stipe down the middle.

Turning our attention to the photographs taken of surgeons, we can visualize a wide range of uniforms and headgear. Most of these uniforms were made by tailors employed by the surgeons. Since the regulations were not ironclad, a variety appeared. In Illust. 188 and 189, the texture of the uniform material is intriguing. It has a shiny surface. Most of the uniforms were made of wool, but perhaps a type of garbadine was also used. There could have been a summer-weight uniform worn also.

In Illust. 185, 186, and 190 there are examples of the medical officer's sword. This type of sword is shown in great detail in Illust. 157 and 158. This particular sword belonged to Surgeon James Fitzpatrick of the 9th Mass. Vol. Inf. It measures 85 cm in length with a very ornate handle, blade and scabbard. Most of the swords have the silver MS on the handle. This again designated medical staff. Illust. 185 shows a sword that was carried by Surgeon McMeens. The handle appears different and it may have an ivory insert. Since Surgeon McMeens died after the Battle of Perryville (October, 1862), this may have been an early type of sword. These swords were carried for ceremony and were probably not found on the battlefield.

Since the surgeon travelled by horseback, he would have worn gauntlets. Illust. 144 shows the gauntlets worn by Surgeon Fitzpatrick. Gauntlets can also be seen in Illust. 187. This particular CVD also shows a surgeon's overcoat with cape.

The uniform of the hospital steward was the single-breasted frock coat with nine buttons (Illust. 191). The insignia worn by the steward on his sleeve was the medical Caduceus on a green field. In Illust. 192 a faint image of the Caduceus can be seen on the right sleeve. From the "Hospital Steward's Manual" written in 1863 by Assistant Surgeon Woodward, the uniform is detailed. "The uniform of the hospital steward consists of:

1. Uniform coat, which is a dark-blue, single-breasted frock, the same as that prescribed by army regulations for all enlisted footmen; except that the cord or welt of cloth which edges the cuffs and collars is crimson, instead of sky blue as for infantry, or yellow as for engineers.

2. Trousers of dark blue cloth, with a stripe of crimson, lace one and one-half inch wide down and over the outer seam.

3. Hat, a black felt hat, the same as that of all enlisted men. The cord of buff and green mixed, the wreath in front of brass, the letters U.S. in Roman of white metal. Brim to be looped up to one side of hat with brass eagle, having a hook attached to the bottom to secure the brim. The feather to be worn on the side opposite the loop.

4. Cravat or stock, black leather, the same as that of all enlisted men.

5. Boots or shoes, the same issued to all enlisted men.

6. Sash, "redworsted" sash, with worsted bullion fringe ends; to go twice around the waist, and to tie behind the left hip, pendant part not to be extended more than 18 inches below the tie.

7. Swordbelt and plate, the same as for all non-commissioned officers.

8. Sword, the same as for all non-commissioned officers.

9. Chevrons, "a half chevron of the following description, viz: of emerald green cloth, one and three fourths inches wide, running obliquely downward from the outer to the inner seam of the sleeve, and at an angle of about 30 degrees with a horizontal, parallel to and 1/8 of an inch distant from both the upper and lower edge, an embroidery of yellow silk 1/8 of an inch wide and in the center a Caduceus 2 inches long, embroidered also with yellow silk and the head towards the outer seam of the sleeve."

To indicate service, the additional half chevrons allowed for all non-commissioned officers, viz., at the expiration of five years service, a diagonal half chevron 1/2 inch wide, to be worn upon both sleeves of the uniform coat, below the elbow, extending from seam to seam, the front and nearest the cuff, and 1/2 inch above the point of the cuff, to be the same color as the edging of the coat (crimson). In like manner, an additional half chevron, above and parallel to the first, for every subsequent five years of faithful service. Distance between each chevron — 1/4 of an inch.

10. Overcoat, the same as for enlisted men.

11. Gloves—on full dress occasions, white cotton gloves should be worn.

12. Scales—on each shoulder of the uniform coat is worn a metallic scale, the same as worn by all non-commissioned officers and enlisted men."[1]

It is a shame that there is no such description of the medical officer's uniform listed in the medical regulations. If we look to the General Regulations of 1861 we find uniform codes for commissioned officers. Regulation #1442 states that all officers shall wear a frock coat of dark blue cloth, the skirt to extend from two-thirds to three-fourths of the distance from the top of the hip to the bend of the knee; single-breasted for Captains and Lieutenants; double-breasted for all other grades. Regulation #1452 states that medical cadets shall wear the uniform the same as that of a Brevet Second Lieutenant.[2]

The buttons for medical officers were the same as for staff officers. Regulation #1460 demands that these buttons be gilt, convex, with spread eagle and stars, and plain border; large size 7/8 inch in exterior diameter; small size 1/2 inch in diameter. Regulation #1466 states that buttons for medical cadets will be the same as for officers of the general staff.[3]

The trousers for staff officers were to be dark blue cloth, with gold cord 1/8 inch in diameter, along the outer seam. Medical cadets were to have the same, but the cord down the seam would be "a welt of buff cloth instead of a gold cord."[4]

Hat trimmings or insignia for the medical department would be the same as for general officers. There would be a gold embroidered wreath in front, on a black velvet ground, encircling the letters U.S. in silver, old English characters. The hat cord would be of black silk and gold.[5] The hat insignia for hospital stewards would be a "cord of buff and green mixed. The wreath in front of brass, with letters U.S. in Roman, of white metal."[6]

The sash as set down in Regulation #1505 would be "medium or emerald green silk net, with silk bullion fringe ends; to go around the waist and tie as general officers'."[7]

The pattern for the sword of the medical officer would be a "small sword and scabbard, according to the pattern of the Surgeon General's office."[8]

The epaulettes for the medical officer would be the same as for the general officer except there would be a laurel wreath embroidered in gold and the letters MS in Old English Characters in silver within the wreath.[9]

The last item mentioned is the shoulder straps, and this causes controversy. There is no mention of the medical officer's straps. There is mention of a strap for a medical cadet. Regulation #1547 states that there will be a strip of gold lace 3 inches long, 1/2 inch wide, placed in the middle of a strap of green cloth 3 3/4 inches long by 1 1/4 inches wide.[10] Why there is no mention of the straps for the medical officer is a mystery. The identifying straps with MS on them cloud the picture also. So the debate will continue among medical collectors until someone comes up with a shoulder strap with a green color and the MS letters on it.

Illust. 144

Union Surgeon's frock coat with sash, medical officer's staff sword and gauntlets belonging to James W. Fitzpatrick of the 9th Mass., Vols. He was mustered in on Aug. 14, 1862 and was discharged on March 29, 1863 to accept a promotion in the Corps of Surgeons, U.S. Vols.

Illust. 145
Surgeon's frock coat which belonged to Maj. Wm. S. Newton, O.V.I. This coat
has green trim and shoulder bars.
From the collection of James Brady, II.

Illust. 146
Medical officers slouch hat with hat cords and "U.S." embroidered insignia. The
color is midnight blue.

Illust. 147

Officer's kepie with gold embroidered "MS" hat insignia. The kepie belonged to Maj. Wm. S. Newton, O.V.I. From the collection of James Brady, II.

Illust. 148 UNION SURGEON'S VEST

Grey in color with 6 staff officers buttons. There are four front pockets and the original brass adjusting buckle on the back. This vest came from the Estate of Surgeon Geo. Rex, 73rd Penna. Vols.

Illust. 149

Emerald green medical officer's sash that belonged to Maj. Wm. S. Newton, O.V.I. From the collection of James Brady, II.

Illust. 150 CONFEDERATE
MEDICAL OFFICER'S FROCK
COAT WITH SASH

From the collection of Dr. Thomas
Wheat.

Illust. 151 SHOULDER STRAPS

These belonged to J. Fitzpatrick, Surgeon of the 9th Mass. Infantry. They are 1st Lt. of Asst. Surgeon straps. They measure 11 cm×4.5 cm. There is silver bullion on midnight blue velvet.

Illust. 152 SHOULDER STRAPS

These were used by a 1st Lt. of the Medical Corps (Assistant Surgeon). The border was of gold bullion thread on a dark blue field. There is a controversy as to the color of the field. Since green was the designated color of the Medical Service, there are instances of the color being green. This particular set is dark or midnight blue. This was the color of a staff officer. Probably the green color was utilized later in the War and that blue was the color used in earlier stages. The English script MS stands for Medical Service. The strap measures 8 cm×3.5 cm.

Illust. 153   GENERAL STAFF BUTTON

This is a close-up of a General Staff button worn on the coat of an army surgeon. It is 2.2 cm in diameter.

Illust. 154   HAT INSIGNIA

This is a close-up of a hat insignia worn by a member of the Medical Service. There is gold bullion thread on a dark blue field. The "US" stands for Medical Staff. The insignia measures 3.5 cm in diameter.

Illust. 155   MEDICAL DEPT. HAT INSIGNIA

Illust. 156   HAT INSIGNIA

Silver bullion thread on a field of midnight blue. The script "MS" stands for Medical Staff.

Illust. 157 POMMEL SHOWING
EAGLE INSERT

Illust. 158 ENGLISH SCRIPT
INSERT (MS) FOR MEDICAL
STAFF

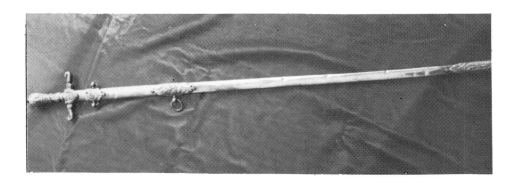

Illust. 159 MEDICAL OFFICER'S STAFF SWORD

Illust. 160 **MEDICAL OFFICER'S SWORD KNOT**

Deep green in color.

Illust. 161

Grouping of items belonging to a surgeon of the 78th Pennsylvania whose identity is unknown. The items left to right and counterclockwise are: Uniform buttons, shoulder insignia, hat cords, shoulder insignia, GAR buttons, cuff buttons.

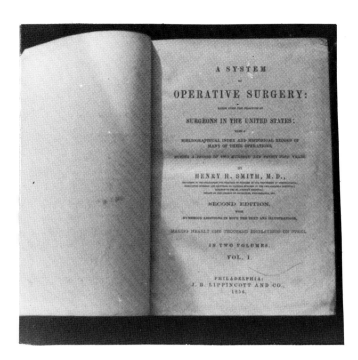

Illust. 162

A two volume text on the subject of Operative Surgery, written by Henry Smith, M.D. in 1856. These volumes contain many illustrations dealing with surgical procedures used during the Civil War. They also contain illustrations of most of the surgical instruments of the period.

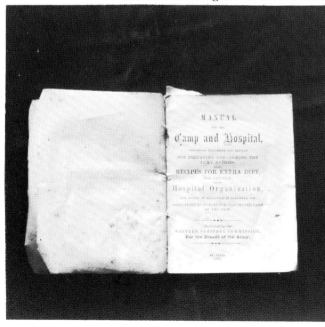

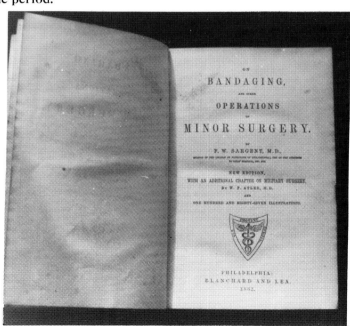

Illust. 163

A manual for preparing food and hospital organization. It was printed by the Western Sanitary Commission. The date of printing was 1862.

Illust. 164

A medical manual of bandaging and minor surgical procedures printed in 1862. It was written by F.W. Sargent, M.D.

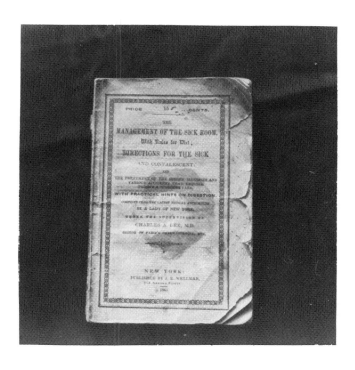

Illust. 165

Medical pamphlet dealing with the subject of sick room management. Printed in 1845.

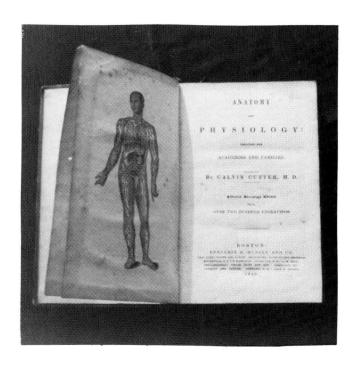

Illust. 166

Medical textbook from the Civil War era. The text is entitled Anatomy & Physiology by Calvin Cutter, M.D. It was printed in 1848.

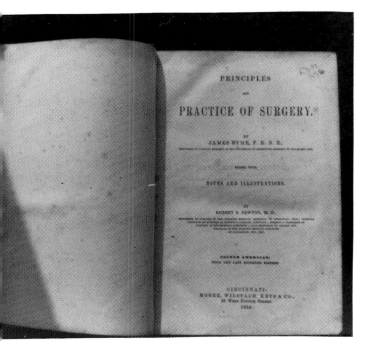

Illust. 167

Medical textbook on the subject of Surgical Practices by James Syme, F.R.S.E. Syme was Professor of Clinical Surgery at the University of Edinburgh. The book was printed in 1858.

Illust. 168

A monumental textbook by former Surgeon General Wm. Hammond, M.D. It was printed by Lippincott & Co. in 1863.

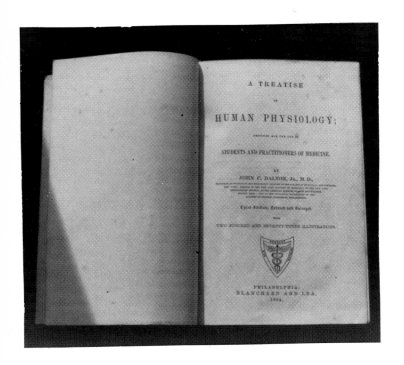

Illust. 169

Civil War Medical textbook on the subject of Human Physiology by John C. Dalton Jr., M.D. It was printed in 1864. The outer cover is marked U.S.A. Hospital Department.

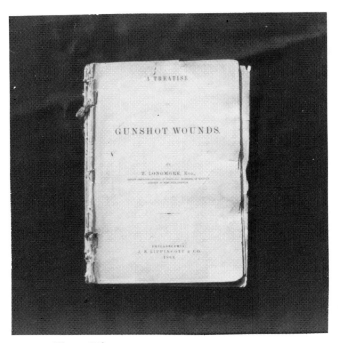

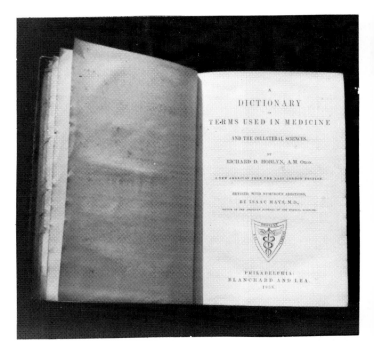

Illust. 170

Medical pamphlet on Gunshot Wounds by T. Longmore, Esq. Longmore was Deputy Inspector General of Hospitals and Professor of Military Surgery at Fort Pitt, Chatam, England. The pamphlet was printed in 1862.

Illust. 171

Medical Dictionary from the Civil War era by Richard D. Hoblyn, A.M., 1858.

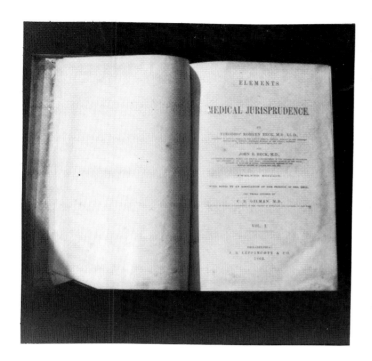

Illust. 172

Textbook on the subject of Medical Jurisprudence by C.R. Gilman, M.D. printed in 1863. The binding is marked U.S.A. Hosp. Dept.

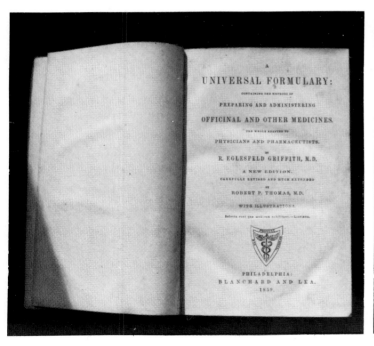

Illust. 173

Medical textbook from the Civil War era. Universal Formulary by R. Eglesfeld Griffith, M.D., 1859.

Illust. 174

Medical textbook from the Civil War era. Urinary Deposits, Diagnosis & Pathology by Golding Bird, M.D., 1859.

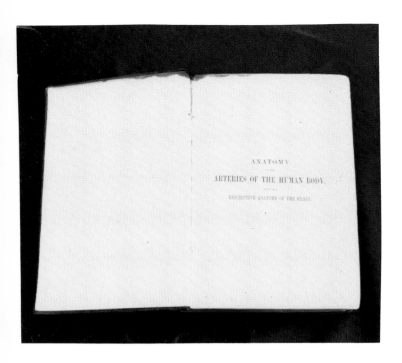

Illust. 175

U.S. Army Medical Text of the Civil War period. This text deals with the arteries of the human body and was written in 1862 by John Hatch Power, M.D. It was authorized by the Sugeon General of the U.S.A. for use in Field and General Hospitals. It was published by J.B. Lippincott and Co. of Philadelphia.

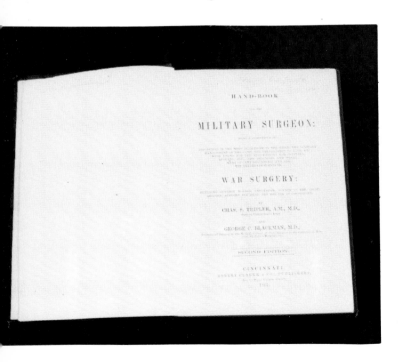
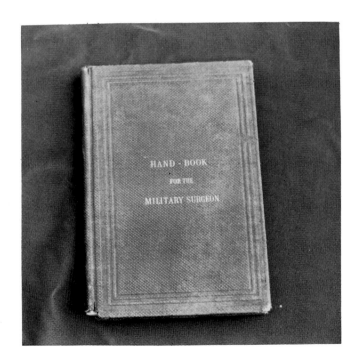

Illust. 176

Military Medical text of the Civil War. This book was written by Chas. S. Tripler, M.D. and George C. Blackman, M.D. It was a compendium of the Duties of the Medical Officer both in the field and in the hospital. It was published in 1861 by Robert Clarke & Co. of Cincinnati.

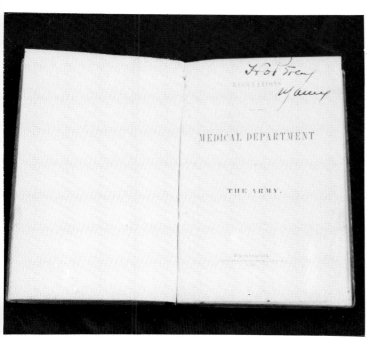

Illust. 177

Text of the Regulations of the Medical Department of the United States Army.
Printed in Washington, D.C. in 1863.

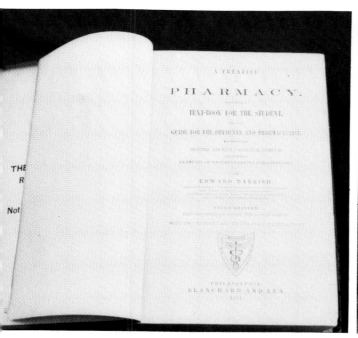

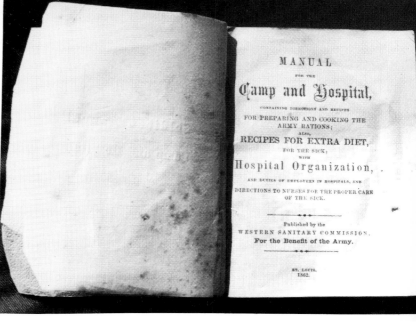

**Illust. 178   TEXTBOOK ON
PHARMACY DATED 1864**

This book was written by Edward Parrish who was Principal of the School of Pharmacy, Philadelphia, Pa. It is illustrated with 258 pictures and it covers most of the knowledge of the time in the field of drug therapy.

Illust. 179

Booklet written by the Western Sanitary Commission for use by soldiers. This booklet was captioned "Manual for the Camp and Hospital" and it contained data or directions for nurses in the proper care of the sick.

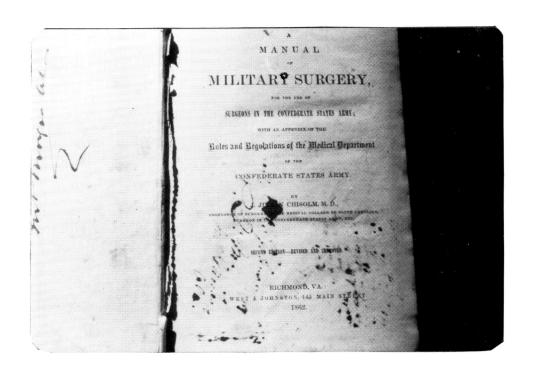

Illust. 180

Manual for Military Surgeons of the Confederate States of America. This manual was written by J. Julian Chisolm, M.D., in 1862.

Illust. 181

A Manual of Military Surgery by J. Julian Chisolm, M.D. with his picture. From the collection of Dr. Thomas Wheat.

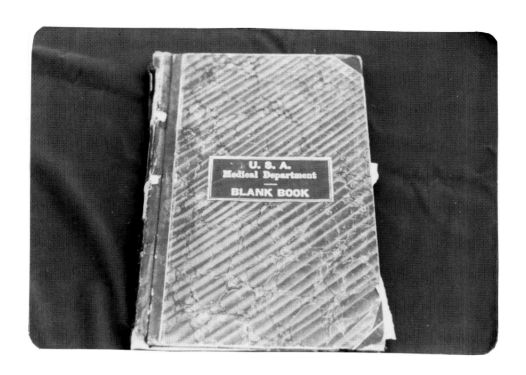

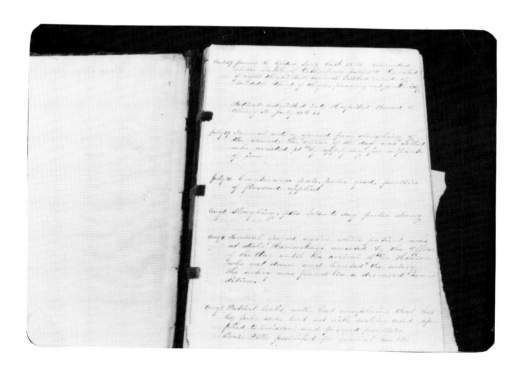

Illust. 182 HOSPITAL DAY BOOK

This book was used at General Hospital, Baltimore, Maryland on Broad and Cherry St. Ward A. The patients were for the most part wounded at the Battle of Gettysburg in July of 1863.

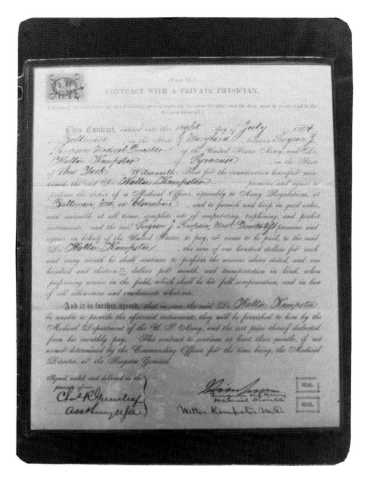

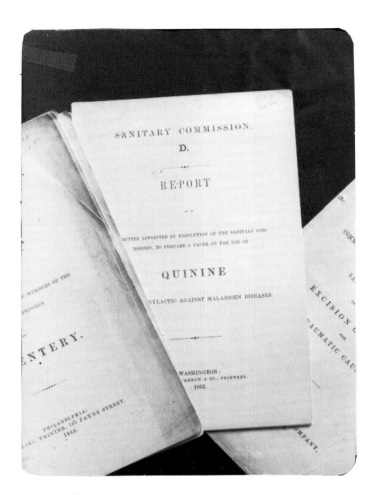

Illust. 183

Document appointing a private physician as a contract surgeon. This was a civilian who was paid by the U.S. Government to attend to the wounded.

Illust. 184

Written reports published by the U.S. Sanitary Commission. These dealt with Disease, Surgery and Hospital Care.

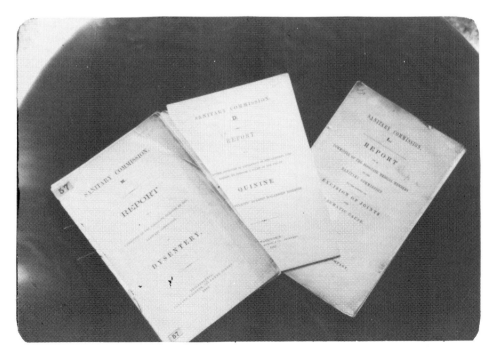

Illust. 185

Identified Albumen of Surgeon R. McMeens, 3rd Ohio. Also is pictured a railroad pass issued to Surgeon McMeens.

Illust. 186

Surgeon John W. Foye of the 11th Mass. Vol. Infantry.

Illust. 187

Unidentified Union Surgeon with overcoat and cape.

Illust. 188

Unidentified Union Surgeon.

Illust. 189
Surgeon J.R. Zearling of the 55th Ill. Vol. Infantry.

Illust. 190
Unidentified Union Surgeon with single breasted frock coat, medical staff sword, medical sash, and kepie with clear picture of insignia.
From the collection of James Brady, II.

Jacob Nebrich
Hospital Steward
2nd Div. 5th Army Corps.
1863

Illust. 191
CDV of Hospital Steward Jacob Nebrich.

Illust. 192
Tin-type of unidentified Union Hospital Steward. From the collection of James Brady, II.

Illust. 193 WOODEN STRETCHER-BED COMBINATION

HOSPITAL SHIP *NASHVILLE*
Courtesy: Illinois State Historical Library

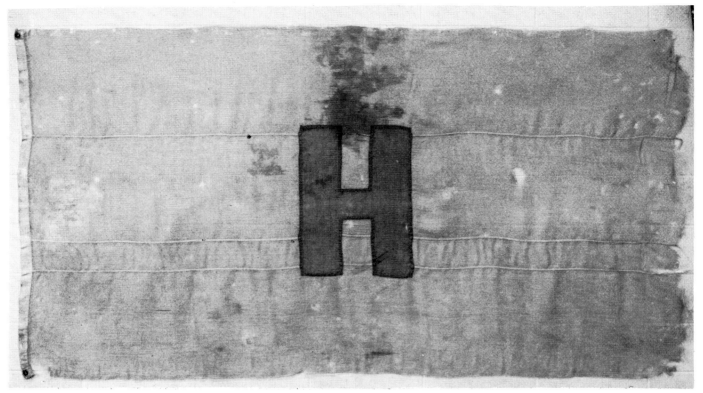

HOSPITAL FLAG
Yellow background with green H. Belonged to surgeon Robert Longhran, 20th New York.
Courtesy: Seward R. Osborne

FOOTNOTES

Chapter 1: Surgical

1. Sanitary Commission Report on the Subject of Amputations, David Clapp Printer, Boston, 1861, p. 3-5.
2. Carver, Eric, M.D., Orthopaedics During the Civil War, p. 3.
3. Chisholm, J. Julian, M.D., A Manual of Military Surgery, West & Johnston, Richmond, Va., 1862, p. 424.
4. Carver, Eric, M.D., Ibid., p. 6.
5. Hamilton, Frank Hastings, M.D., A Treatise on Military Surgery and Hygiene, Bailliere Brothers, New York, 1865, p. 421.
6. Chisolm, J. Julian, M.D., Ibid., p. 427.
7. Nevius, Laird, W., M.D., The Discovery of Modern Anaesthesia, Cooper Institute, New York, 1894, p. 65.
8. Syme, James, F.R.S.E., Principles and Practice of Surgery, Moore, Wilstach, Keys & Co., Cincinnati, 1858, p. 720.
9. Syme, James, F.R.S.E., Ibid., p. 721.
10. Chisolm, J. Julian, Ibid., p. 49.
11. Sanitary Commission Report on the Subject of Excision of Joints, Welch, Bigelow, and Company, Cambridge, 1862, p. 2.

12. Warren, Edward, M.D., An Epitome of Practical Surgery for Field and Hospital, West & Johnston, Richmond, 1863, p. 179.
13. Chisolm, J. Julian, Ibid., p. 431.
14. Carver, Eric, M.D., Ibid., p. 5.
15. Hamilton, Frank Hastings, M.D., Ibid., p. 479.
16. Hamilton, Frank Hastings, M.D., Ibid., p. 184.
17. Hamilton, Frank Hastings, M.D., Ibid., p. 197.
18. Smith, Henry H., A System of Operative Surgery, J.B. Lippincott and Co., Philadelphia, 1856, p. 222.
19. Hamilton, Frank Hastings, M.D., Ibid., p. 217.
20. Chisolm, J. Julian, Ibid., p. 223.
21. Chisolm, J. Julian, Ibid., p. 225.

Chapter 2: War on Disease

1. Hamilton, Frank Hastings, M.D., A Treatise on Military Surgery and Hygiene, Bailliere Brothers, New York, 1865, p. 567.
2. Ibid., p. 579.
3. Parrish, Edward, A Treatise on Pharmacy, Blanchard and Lea, Philadelphia, 1864, p. 642.
4. Sanitary Commission Report on Quinine, McGill, Witherow & Co., Washington, 1862, p. 6.

5. Parrish, Edward, Ibid., p. 643.

6. Ibid., p. 480.

7. Brooks, Stewart, Civil War Medicine, Charles C. Thomas Publisher, Springfield, 1966, p. 20.

8. Ibid., p. 130.

Chapter 5: Medical Insignia and Uniforms

1. Woodward, Joseph Janvier, M.D., The Hospital Steward's Manual, J.B. Lippincott & Co., Philadelphia, 1863, pp. 25-28.

2. Revised Regulations for the Army of the United States, War Dept., J.G.L. Brown - Printer, Philadelphia, 1861, p. 477.

3. Ibid., p. 479.

4. Ibid., p. 479.

5. Ibid., p. 480.

6. Ibid., p. 481.

7. Ibid., p. 482.

8. Ibid., p. 483.

9. Ibid., p. 484.

10. Ibid., p. 486.

BIBLIOGRAPHY

Adams, George W., Doctors in Blue, New York, Henry Schuman, 1952.

Brooks, Stewart, Civil War Medicine, Springfield, Charles C. Thomps, 1966.

Cunningham, Horace H., Doctors in Gray, Baton Rouge, Louisiana State University Press, 1958.

Carver, Eric, M.D., Orthopaedics During the Civil War.

Chisholm, J. Julian, M.D., A Manual of Military Surgery, Richmond, West: Johnston, 1862.

Hamilton, Frank Hastings, A Treatise on Military Surgery, New York, Bailliere Bros., 1865.

Hammond, William A. M.D., Lectures on Venereal Diseases, Philadelphia, J.R. Lippincott & Co., 1864.

Longmore, T., Esq., A Treatise on Gunshot Wounds, Philadelphia, J.B. Lippincott & Co., 1862.

Neill, John, M.D.; Smith, Francis, M.D., An Analytical Compendium of the Various Branches of Medical Science, Philadelphia, Blanchard and Lea, 1856.

Nevius, Laird W., The Discovery of Anaesthesia, New York, Cooper Institute, 1894.

Parrish, Edward, A Treatise on Pharmacy, Philadelphia, Blanchard and Lea, 1864.

Perkins, Henry C., M.D., An Article of the Physician and Surgeon in War, Read at the annual meeting May 29, 1861.

Regulations for the Medical Department of the Army, Washington, A.O.P. Nicholson - Printer, 1856.

Revised Regulations for the Army of the United States, Philadelphia, J.G.L. Brown - Publisher, 1861.

Sanitary Commission Report on Amputations, Boston, David Clapp - Printer, 1861.

Sanitary Commission Report on the Treatment of Fractures in Military Surgery, Philadelphia, J.B. Lippincott & Co., 1862.

Sanitary Commission Report on Quinine, Washington, McGill, Witherow & Co., - Printer, 1862.

Sanitary Commission Report on the Excision of Joints, Cambridge, Welch, Bigelow and Company, 1862.

Sargent, F.W., M.D., On Bandaging and Other Operations of Minor Surgery, Philadelphia, Blanchard and Lea, 1862.

Scudder, John M., M.D., The Eclectic Practice of Medicine, Cincinnati, Moore, Wilstach, Keys & Co., 1864.

Smith, George W., Medicines for the Union Army, Madison, American Institute of the History of Pharmacy, 1962.

Smith, Henry H., A System of Operative Surgery, Philadelphia, J.B. Lippincott and Co., 1856.

Syme, James, Principles and Practical Surgery, Cincinnati, Moore, Wilstach, Keys & Co., 1858.

Warren, Edward, M.D., An Epitome of Practical Surgery for Field and Hospital, Richmond, West & Johnston, 1863.

Woodward, Joseph Janvier, M.D., The Hospital Steward's Manual, Philadelphia, J.B. Lippincott & Co., 1863.

Woodward, Joseph Janvier, M.D., Outlines of the Chief Camp Diseases of the United States Armies, Philadelphia, J.B. Lippincott & Co., 1863.

ABOUT THE AUTHOR

Dr. Gordon E. Dammann, a graduate of Loyola University, Chicago, Illinois, and Loyola University School of Dentistry, maintains a private practice of dentistry in Lena, Illinois. In addition to his historical interests he is an N.C.A.A. and Illinois High School football official. He lives in Lena, Illinois, with his wife, Karen, and two sons, Greg and Doug.